EMOTIONAL INTELLIGENCE

50 Lessons on Knowing Who You're Dealing With

Joe Serio, Ph.D.

To Juanita —

Move from the inside out!

Best wishes! Joe

Copyright © 2017

No part of this publication may be transmitted in any form or by any means, electronic, mechanical, photocopying, recording, scanning, or by an information storage and retrieval system, or otherwise, except as permitted under Sections 107 or 108 of the 1976 U.S. Copyright Act, without the prior written consent of the Publisher.

This publication is designed to provide accurate and authoritative information in regard to the subject matter covered. It is sold with the understanding that neither the Author nor the Publisher is engaged in rendering legal, accounting, financial or other professional services. If legal advice or other expert assistance is required, the services of a competent professional should be sought. Neither the Publisher nor the Author shall be liable for damages, directly or indirectly, arising herefrom.

Design Team: Harriet McHale and Tracey Neikirk

Printed in the United States of America
ISBN 13: 978-0-9981642-2-9

www.joeserio.com

Contents

ABOUT THE GET THE NERVE™ SERIES   7

INTRODUCTION   10

PART 1
THE BASICS   13

Lesson 1:	Emotional Intelligence	14
Lesson 2:	Pillar 1: Self-Awareness	16
Lesson 3:	Three Cornerstone Questions for Self-Awareness	18
Lesson 4:	My Lack of Self-Awareness: Trying to Be the Hero	20
Lesson 5:	Pillar 2: Self-Management	22
Lesson 6:	Vinnie's Temper	24
Lesson 7:	Pillar 3: Social Awareness	26
Lesson 8:	You're Only Human	28
Lesson 9:	Pillar 4: Relationship Management	30
Lesson 10:	Pulling Pins and Throwing Grenades	32
Lesson 11:	Components of Emotional Intelligence	34
Lesson 12:	What People with High EI Do	36
Lesson 13:	Do You Need to Improve Your EI?	38

PART 2
FEAR AND EI   41

Lesson 14:	Fear	42
Lesson 15:	The Fear List	44
Lesson 16:	Fear of Public Speaking	46

Lesson 17:	Expectations and Reality	48
Lesson 18:	Handling Fear	50
Lesson 19:	Moving Forward	52

PART 3
INSIDE YOUR BRAIN 55

Lesson 20:	Reptilian Brain	56
Lesson 21:	The Amygdala	58
Lesson 22:	The Prefrontal Cortex	60
Lesson 23:	The Amygdala and Prefrontal Cortex Battle	62
Lesson 24:	Fight, Flight, Freeze…or a Different Way	64

PART 4
MAKING THE RIGHT CHOICES 67

Lesson 25:	The Chinese Farmer	68
Lesson 26:	E + R = O	70
Lesson 27:	Triggers and Hot Buttons	72
Lesson 28:	Pulling the Right Lever	74
Lesson 29:	The Invisible Spectrum	76
Lesson 30:	Putting It All Together	78

PART 5
RESILIENCE AND EI 81

Lesson 31:	Resilience	82
Lesson 32:	Resilience Inventory	84
Lesson 33:	Choose the Story of Your Life Wisely	86
Lesson 34:	Take Charge of Your Life	88
Lesson 35:	Thinking in Advance	90
Lesson 36:	Re-telling Your Story	92

PART 6
IMPROVING YOUR EI 95

Lesson 37:	EI and Stress	96
Lesson 38:	Stay Out of Your Thinking Traps	98
Lesson 39:	The Daily Thought Record	100
Lesson 40:	Silence Your Inner Critic	102
Lesson 41:	What You Focus On Expands	104
Lesson 42:	Laugh Whenever You Can	106
Lesson 43:	Move to Improve EI	108
Lesson 44:	Be a Sleeping Beauty	110
Lesson 45:	Breathe	112
Lesson 46:	Learn to Say No	114
Lesson 47:	Love the Plateau	116
Lesson 48:	7 Steps to Emotional Intelligence	118
Lesson 49:	The 7 Habits of Highly Effective People	120
Lesson 50:	Mindfulness	122

THE ROAD AHEAD 124

THE TAKEAWAYS 126

BIOGRAPHY 130

The long span of the bridge of your life is supported by countless cables called habits, attitudes, and desires. What you do in life depends upon what you are and what you want. What you get from life depends upon how much you want it, how much you are willing to work and plan and cooperate and use your resources. The long span of the bridge of your life is supported by countless cables that you are spinning now, and that is why today is such an important day. Make the cables strong!

~ L.G. Elliott

About the *Get the Nerve*™ Series

The idea for the *Get the Nerve*™ *Series* grew out of my personal transformation from being fearful of most things to facing that fear and achieving more than I thought possible.

My goal is to share what I have learned so that you, too, can see the possibility for your own life and make it a reality.

Each book in the series begins with reflections on fear. This builds the foundation for the following lessons, which are specific to the topic of each book. As L.G. Elliott says in the quotation on the facing page, "Your life is supported by countless cables called habits, attitudes, and desires." This series is a blueprint for helping you create and strengthen the cables of your bridge, so you can live the most inspired life you can imagine.

I would love to hear about changes you make in your life as a result of the *Get the Nerve*™ *Series*. Please contact me with your stories of personal transformation at joe@joeserio.com.

Other Titles in the Get the Nerve™ Series

Overcoming Fear: 50 Lessons on Being Bold and Living the Dream

Time Management: 50 Lessons on Finding Time for What's Important

Public Speaking: 50 Lessons on Presenting Without Losing Your Cool

Effective Communication: 50 Lessons on How to Hear and Be Heard

Leadership: 50 Lessons on Inspiring Others to Be Their Best

Being Resilient: 50 Lessons on Leaving Chronic Stress Behind

Introduction

*For usually and fitly, the presence of an introduction
is held to imply that there is something of
consequence and importance to be introduced.*

~ Arthur Machen

Emotional intelligence lies at the core of your life.

It drives what you believe to be true about yourself and what you think of the world around you.

It dramatically influences your behavior and the quality of your relationships.

It impacts every area of your life.

Basically, emotional intelligence is about understanding yourself and taking time to understand others, hence, the subtitle of this book: *50 Lessons on Knowing Who You're Dealing With*. Do you have the courage to face the facts about your life? Are you willing to slow down long enough to understand others?

Here's an important fact to understand early on in our journey: it's very simple to understand the basics of emotional intelligence. You can get the gist of it in just a few minutes.

The more difficult part is getting inside yourself, exploring where you are, how you got there, and where you're headed.

The faster you commit to making the necessary changes in your life, the faster you will see results you never dreamed possible.

The vast majority of this book will focus on understanding how emotional intelligence shows up in your life, what it looks like, how it's important, and tools and techniques for improving your emotional intelligence.

The price to pay for having low emotional intelligence can be very high, indeed. I recently came across the following list called, Top 5 Regrets of the Dying, by Bronnie Ware, which reminded me of what's at stake.

All five of these regrets are intimately connected to emotional intelligence.

1. I wish I'd had the courage to live a life true to myself, not the life others expected of me.
2. I wish I hadn't worked so hard.
3. I wish I'd had the courage to express my feelings.
4. I wish I had stayed in touch with my friends.
5. I wish I had let myself be happier.

You may see something of yourself in this list. Perhaps one of the main questions you have to concern yourself with is: How many regrets do you want to have when you get to the end of your road?

How to Use This Book

Emotional Intelligence: 50 Lessons on Knowing Who You're Dealing With is a practical guide of tools and techniques to help you improve your emotional intelligence and get more of what you want out of life.

This book is arranged in six parts:

Part 1, The Basics, outlines the four pillars as well as the three components of emotional intelligence. You'll have a chance to see if you need to improve your emotional intelligence. Part 1 is the foundation for the rest of the book.

Part 2, Fear and EI, addresses the issue of fear, the primary reason people don't get what they want. There is a very close symbiotic relationship between fear and emotional intelligence. Addressing one helps deal with the other.

Part 3, Inside Your Brain, looks at very fundamental brain function. It's critical to understand how your brain is influencing your emotions and your decision making and how it can keep you from getting great outcomes in your life.

Part 4, Making the Right Choices, takes the information from the first three parts of the book and shows how you can manage yourself and your decision making better. This part provides a framework for facing any difficult situation and getting good results.

Part 5, Resilience and EI, discusses your ability to bounce back from adversity, a difficult past, bad relationships, and other challenges. Resilience is part of the core of emotional intelligence and is critical to your future success.

Part 6, Improving Your EI, provides additional tools and techniques that have been proven to improve emotional intelligence. These practices and exercises in this part are simple, straightforward, and effective.

Emotional Intelligence is meant to be read from beginning to end. The information presented here is cumulative, building on everything that comes before it.

Master the lessons in this book and you will gain clarity about what's important to you and how to get more of it. Your life will change and the future will be brighter when you put into practice the kinds of recommendations presented throughout the book.

Part 1

The Basics

Lesson 1
Emotional Intelligence

Freedom is the will to be responsible for ourselves.
~ Friedrich Neitzsche

*It is better to conquer yourself than to
win a thousand battles.*
~ Buddha

The quality of your life is determined in large measure by the mind and heart you bring to the hundreds of situations you encounter daily.

Do you bury your feelings rather than acknowledge and understand them? Are you hanging on to anger and fear, letting them dictate your behavior? Do you fly off the handle easily? Do you eat excessively out of nervousness?

What state are your relationships in? Are you quick to judge, criticize, complain, and blame others in order to make yourself feel better? Do you try to manipulate others in order to maintain control over them?

Are you getting married, buying a house, or having children because of peer pressure, because it's expected of you? Do you hate your job but are too scared to leave it? Have you been divorced multiple times?

Do you realize that your emotions — and your level of emotional intelligence — are the drivers behind all of these behaviors?

Your outcomes in life are often determined by what you think, believe, and feel is possible.

What you feel and think is possible derives largely from what you think is true about yourself.

And what you think is true about yourself often comes out, whether your realize it or not, in how you see the world around you.

Think about the outcomes you're getting in your life. How and why do you choose to do the things you do? Are you chasing things that ultimately don't add to your life but rather subtract from it? Are you good about getting what you really need or are you protecting yourself from potential pain and in the process missing your best life?

For purposes of this book, emotional intelligence is defined as your ability to be aware of, understand, manage, and express your own emotions and understand the emotions of others.

Then, you use that information to guide your thinking and behavior for good outcomes in your self-development and in your relationships with others. Emotional intelligence is abbreviated as either EI or EQ (emotional quotient).

The four basic pillars of EI are:
1. Self-Awareness
2. Self-Management
3. Social Awareness
4. Relationship Management

The order listed above is critical. You always begin with yourself. You work on yourself first before expecting or demanding that others change.

You won't be able to improve the outcomes in your life significantly until you begin to understand your own emotions, beliefs, and thoughts that led to your actions.

At the end of one of my EI trainings, one of the participants approached me and said, "I got divorced three months ago and now I realize that I was the jerk in the relationship." At that moment, he was ready to start exploring his emotional intelligence instead of blaming others for the way his life turned out.

TAKEAWAY: Emotional intelligence drives the outcomes you get in life.

Lesson 2
Pillar 1: Self-Awareness

Know thyself.
> ~ Oracle at Delphi

*To find the courage within you,
give up the quest to become fearless.
Concentrate instead on being fear-conscious.*
> ~ Sarah Quigley

You, as an individual, are the starting point, and self-awareness is the foundation of all personal change.

It's of little use to require that everyone else change in order for you to be happy, to get more of what you want in life, to become more of who you can be. It begins with you.

Self-awareness is the critical ingredient without which everything else will be far more difficult.

Self-awareness asks you to focus on "What's going on inside of me at this moment?" It means suspending judgment of yourself and others for a time while you reflect on what is *actually going on* rather than what you *think should be.*

People high in self-awareness are practiced at perceiving their own emotions in the moment and know their typical reactions to specific events, challenges, and people. They also know their own triggers and have worked out their responses to those triggers.

They get to know themselves under stress; they pursue the right opportunities; they don't let their emotions be an obstacle in their lives. They know their strengths and their weaknesses, and they know what makes them tick.

Those high in self-awareness are good at saying no. They have identified their emotions, feelings, and beliefs. They have established their priorities based on their values and set and pursue goals with that information in hand. They say yes to the right things and don't allow themselves to be ruled by peer pressure or guilt.

People high in self-awareness know that they must get out of their comfort zone in order to grow, mature, learn new things, and succeed.

Without good self-awareness, you may simply be acting out of habit. You could be on a path that has been largely pre-programmed by others' values and beliefs (parents, church, school, peers).

What if that path isn't what you really want?

Being self-aware encompasses virtually every aspect of your life: your health, exercise, nutrition, weight, money, job, communication style, relationships, and everything else. And they're all connected.

They form a system, and when you change something in one part of your life, it will change one or more things in other parts of your life.

When you are low in self-awareness, it's likely that most aspects of your life are suffering for it. When you begin to explore and improve your self-awareness, you'll start to change the choices you make, which will improve your life.

Keep in mind that improving self-awareness doesn't mean you have to quit your job and go to a mountaintop to become a monk. It's not about holding hands and singing Kumbaya. It's not warm and fuzzy navel gazing.

Self-awareness is a powerful practice that will bring you clarity about what you want, how you want to be, and how you will interact with others. Reflecting on your life will bring you in closer contact with your real self that has been hidden for so long.

TAKEAWAY: Improving your self-awareness is the key first step in moving toward high emotional intelligence.

Lesson 3
Three Cornerstone Questions for Self-Awareness

*I never learn anything talking.
I only learn things when I ask questions.*
> ~ Lou Holtz

*Your mind will answer most questions
if you learn to relax and wait for the answer.*
> ~ William S. Burroughs

The foundation of self-awareness can, for the time being, be boiled down to three cornerstone questions. When you begin to answer these questions, you will start on your road to self-awareness.

1. Who am I?
2. What do I want?
3. How am I going to get it?

These are seemingly simple questions on their surface, especially numbers two and three, but don't be fooled. They're challenging questions that, when answered as fully as possible, will take you on an incredible journey.

They will take you deep inside yourself.

Who am I?

When you pose this question to yourself, you're reflecting largely on your past. Where did you come from? How did your family, friends, religion, and community influence who you are today? What habits, attitudes, values, and beliefs did you inherit from those around you? What assumptions and expectations did you *choose to carry with you as truth* that formed the way you look at yourself? How have these impacted your decisions in life? How do they influence your responses to the world around you today?

What do I want?

This question puts you squarely in the present. It will require some imagination about the future, but you have to begin to answer it before moving on. In the cold light of day, without considering obstacles, without the fear of failure, ask yourself, "What do I want?" The key is to be as specific and detailed (and bold!) as possible and address the major parts of your life: relationships, health, career, finances, and others. When you know who you are and what you want, it will be easier to choose your path ahead, decide who you want in your life, define how you'll spend your time, determine what and how much you will eat, and virtually everything else.

How am I going to get it?

This question is about working today to create your future. This is the stage at which you will strategize, plan, and get to work. You'll come up against obstacles and fears, and you'll have a plan for dealing with them. You will get frustrated. This is when you'll need to remember who you are and what you want. This is where you'll show yourself how badly you want it.

These questions require you to face the brutal facts about who you are, where you are in life, and how the decisions you made got you there. They may require some forgiveness of yourself and others as well as letting go of long-held beliefs that have kept you stuck.

These are not simple questions with easy answers, but it should be clear that they are directly connected to your emotional intelligence. If you don't begin to answer these questions, you may remain locked down in low emotional intelligence, making bad decisions and choices, and living someone else's life instead of your own.

TAKEAWAY: Begin to answer the three cornerstone questions to improve your self-awareness.

Lesson 4

My Lack of Self-Awareness: Trying to Be the Hero

*We are dangerous when we are not conscious of
our responsibility for how we behave, think, and feel.*
∼ Marshall B. Rosenberg

*Self-awareness is the ability to take an honest look
at your life without any attachment to it
being right or wrong, good or bad.*
∼ Debbie Ford

In 1988, I taught at a police academy in Shanghai, China. One day, the school provided a cruise to the Yangtze River. On the outbound leg, one of my colleagues, a 60-year-old American woman, asked me if I wanted to go to the gift shop. I declined. Several hours later, I changed my mind, but I had forgotten the card that foreign workers used to purchase things. My colleague lent me hers.

The only problem was that each card had the person's headshot on it, and I definitely couldn't pass for a 60-year-old woman! I used it anyway figuring that, at worst, the purchase would be rejected.

I picked out some items and handed over the card. The Chinese clerk immediately started yelling at me. Apparently, she didn't think I could pass for a 60-year-old woman, either!

I stood and listened to the woman berate me for 10 minutes. Why didn't I walk away?

The stress built up. I could feel my muscles tightening and my blood pressure increasing. The situation came to the attention of the Chinese representative from the police academy. She rushed in and started yelling at the clerk.

Unwisely, I still stood there, stress levels continuing to rise.

I suddenly got a brilliant idea. Somehow, my elementary school teachers came to mind. I recalled how they would slam a thick textbook on a wooden desk to make a loud noise and shock the chattering students into silence. It seemed to work well so I figured I'd try it.

I didn't have a textbook so I used my hand. I raised my arm and brought my hand down with force. By the way, it wasn't a wooden desk but a glass countertop. I shattered the whole thing! Chips of glass lodged in my hand and blood trickled down my arm.

To add insult to injury, it didn't work! The clerk waved her arm in my direction without skipping a beat as if to say, "Now look what he's done! He's going to pay for that!" Why couldn't I just walk away?

The reason had nothing to do with the situation.

I was thinking I would solve the problem and the clerk would be forced to see what a clever person I was. "This young American is so brilliant!" she would exclaim. "Look at how expertly he resolved this international incident!"

No, this young American was operating from a lack of self-awareness with low emotional intelligence. I was acting out a narrative I'd had from childhood.

I was the 9th in a family of 12 siblings, feeling inadequate, unseen, unacceptable, and lost. Smashing the glass countertop was my way of showing somebody, anybody — even a perfect stranger on the other side of the world — that I was somebody. I was trying to be the hero and save the day, to be seen as clever and smart!

It was the issue that lay beneath that I had to examine and deal with. I had to improve my self-awareness to understand and improve my behavior.

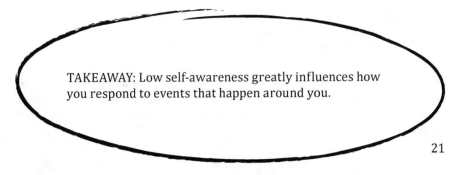

TAKEAWAY: Low self-awareness greatly influences how you respond to events that happen around you.

Lesson 5
Pillar 2: Self-Management

> *I am, indeed, a king,*
> *because I know how to rule myself.*
> ~ Pietro Aretino

> *A person who refuses to manage himself and*
> *discipline his flesh will be disciplined and*
> *taught by life itself.*
> ~ Sunday Adelaja

The second of the four pillars of emotional intelligence is self-management.

Self-management is your ability to use your awareness of your emotions to stay flexible and to direct your behavior properly.

The chain of your thoughts, decisions, and actions lead to some outcome. Generally speaking, good self-management leads to outcomes that are healthy and beneficial; inadequate self-management frequently leads to complications and negative consequences.

So far, we can summarize emotional intelligence as knowing yourself better in order to manage yourself better.

In the Chinese boat example, I had low self-awareness and, therefore, my self-management suffered. I smashed the glass countertop instead of choosing a better, healthier, more productive option.

If you're willing to engage in self-awareness, you can more easily monitor your self-management. For example, when you're more self-aware, it will be easier to see when you may have managed yourself poorly and then take steps to rectify the situation.

As much as I wanted to blame the Chinese cashier, I later had to admit to myself that she did not make me smash the glass.

Self-management — what you do, how you act — becomes much more difficult if you haven't spent any time answering the three cornerstone questions discussed earlier: Who am I? What do I want? How am I going to get it?

Failure to engage in self-awareness and improve your self-management will have a negative effect on one, some, or many parts of your life. If you don't know who you are, how will you know what you stand for? What will you find acceptable and unacceptable?

Fixing one part of your life frequently automatically fixes many other parts. For example, you may fall asleep every night in the recliner in front of the television after eating ice cream and cookies. If you go to bed earlier, before you're wiped out in the recliner, you will likely sleep more comfortably which may lead to being less grumpy in the morning, which can improve your communication style, which may improve your relationships with the people you live with, which will put you in a better mood when you get to work, which can improve your performance, and on and on.

Part of the challenge in your life may be that you're avoiding what you really need to face. Or you're waiting for others to manage themselves better in order for you to be happier, healthier, and more successful.

Or maybe you're waiting for permission from someone to live the life you really want to.

You may be hesitant about moving forward because you're really not sure how to.

You and you alone must take what you learn from improving your self-awareness and apply it to your self-management.

The good news is there are hundreds of opportunities every day to practice.

TAKEAWAY: Use your awareness of yourself to improve your actions and get better results.

Lesson 6
Vinnie's Temper

If you want something you've never had, you must be willing to do something you've never done.
~ Thomas Jefferson

Holding on to anger is like grasping a hot coal with the intent of throwing it at someone else: you are the one who gets burned.
~ Buddha

Vinnie was a participant in my personal leadership series at a major police department. He heard me refer to my father as a Sicilian volcano and said, "Joe, I think you're going to understand my situation very well."

Vinnie, a Sicilian, had a temper that was causing problems in his life. It kept him from being the best husband, father, and detective possible. To his credit, Vinnie was willing to talk about his issues during the classes.

When things didn't go his way, he said, when people didn't behave the way he expected them to, when his kids didn't pay attention, he would explode.

Do you think Vinnie wanted to lose his temper? It was a response he learned watching his own father. He didn't really know any other way.

Vinnie told me that when he got mad, "I clench my fists. The muscles in my arms tighten. My face gets red. And my ears get hot." "And what happens next?" I asked. "I lose my temper," he said. "How many times would you say you lose your temper after you go through that process?" "Every single time." "So, the thousand times that's happened in the past, you exploded a thousand times." "Yep." "It's predictable, then." "Guaranteed."

I asked him several more questions about his values, beliefs, and priorities, and finally said to him, "Why don't you hit the pause button?" "What's that?" "The pause button is a device, a tool, something you can use to change your situation. Do you like losing your temper?" "Of course not," he said.

"So, when you start to clench your fists, you hit the pause button. That means you find a way to slow down the emotions, short circuit your usual reaction process and choose to respond instead of react. It's a way to change your behavior and get what you want. You already know exactly what happens when you lose your temper. It happens the same way every time. So you can pick a spot early on in that process and hit the pause button."

From the look on his face, Vinnie apparently had never considered such a thing. I continued. "The pause button can be anything you want it to be as long as it interrupts what's happening at that moment. You could excuse yourself and say, 'I'd really like to continue this conversation, but I have to go to the men's room. I'll be back in a second.' Then you leave the room and go somewhere to calm down for a minute.

"Or you can count to 10. Or you can ask questions of the person to get more information; maybe you don't have the full story yet. It almost doesn't matter what it is as long as you have a simple, conscious, and constructive way to change your usual reaction."

After just a few weeks with the pause button and other tools, Vinnie started responding to his environment in a more healthy way.

One day, Vinnie's daughter, who also worked in the police department, came to one of my classes. She asked, "What did you do to my father?" I was taken aback. "My father used to have a temper of about 95 out of 100; now it's around 10. He's not perfect but he's so much better than before!"

That's powerful stuff. Can you hit the pause button, count to 10, or excuse yourself before you lose your temper? Or would you exhibit low emotional intelligence, lash out, and continue to get terrible outcomes?

TAKEAWAY: You can change your self-management by hitting the pause button.

Lesson 7
Pillar 3: Social Awareness

Emotions are in charge of our behavior and specifically on how we react to the world around us.
~ John C. Allen

I have striven not to laugh at human actions, not to weep at them, nor to hate them, but to understand them.
~ Baruch Spinoza

The third pillar of emotional intelligence is social awareness. That's increasingly difficult in this era of non-stop technology, distractions, and self-absorption.

Do you do a good job of picking up on other people's emotions? Do you take time to understand what's going on with them? Do you try to understand their perspective? Do you have empathy?

So often, in the course of conversation, you have your own monologue running through your head, anxiously awaiting your turn to speak rather than really being present in that moment. You're often thinking ahead to what you're going to say.

When you do this, you miss important clues about the point the other person is really making, about body language, about subtext, about their state of mind.

Social awareness is a challenge because it means you have to figure out what's happening with the other person or group of people. Even more difficult is that you're doing it while you're in the midst of an interaction with them, juggling your own feelings, assumptions, and perceptions.

Start improving your social awareness by improving your powers of observation. Watch body language, listen more carefully to words and tone, understand people's intentions.

For example, when someone tries to make you feel guilty for something of their own doing, or when you find yourself feeling guilty because of others' expectations of you, it's time to step back, observe, interpret, and understand: "What's really going on here? What is my responsibility here? Am I being maneuvered or manipulated into feeling badly by someone who is unwilling to take responsibility for their own life?"

In my programs I often ask, "What do you see with?" Understandably, most people answer, "My eyes." My response to them is, "You see *through* your eyes; you see *with* your brain."

Often, you see what you want to see, what you expect to see, rather than what's really there. This is conditioned by the way you were raised, what your friends and community told you, the way media has shaped your assumptions and perceptions, and many other factors.

Your eyes can see things but your brain is providing the context, and a different context makes the picture look different. Social awareness requires you to put your context on hold and try to understand where the other person is coming from.

When I was growing up, I interpreted pretty much everything based on the way it made me feel. I believed that other people's bad moods, stress, defensiveness, sarcasm, and everything else were about me.

I concluded that I was inadequate, insufficient, unacceptable, and unlovable. In other words, I had low emotional intelligence.

Over time, I realized I had to improve my own self-awareness and self-management in order to improve my social awareness. I had to reinterpret my childhood experience. I had to understand what was about me and take responsibility for it, and try not to own other peoples emotions.

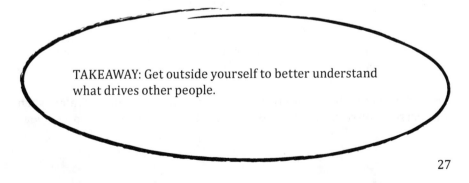

TAKEAWAY: Get outside yourself to better understand what drives other people.

Lesson 8

You're Only Human

*When we get too caught up in the busyness
of the world, we lose connection with one another —
and ourselves.*

~ Jack Kornfield

*Your emotional awareness and abilities to handle
feelings will determine your success and happiness in
all walks of life, including family relationships.*

~ John Gottman

Part of the difficulty with improving social awareness is that you so often forget one useful piece of information: You're human and the people around you are human.

You'll make mistakes and others will make mistakes.

But, life becomes a bit easier when you slow down long enough to understand the realities of the human experience and then create tools and techniques to manage those realities.

Here are two simple examples to illustrate what I mean.

The first example comes from my home life. When my wife and I speak with each other, it happens on occasion that one of us will "zone out" when the other is speaking.

I'm sure you're familiar with this. Indeed, you may get really irritated when the person you're speaking with zones out. You may even express your frustration: "You never listen to me!" Suddenly, the two of you are headed for an argument.

But consider this: With everything you have going on in your life — the distractions, the commitments, the fatigue, the fear and anxiety — isn't it likely that you're going to zone out from time to time?

With the belief that the answer to that question is yes, my wife suggested that the person listening simply stop the person speaking and say, "I'm sorry, I just zoned out for a second. Could you repeat that last thing you said?"

Underlying that request is the idea that the listener didn't zone out on purpose. In this way, the listener can recover quickly and the speaker isn't offended.

The second example is of a husband who is asked by his wife for the first time in months to get a gallon of milk on his way home from work.

When the husband walks in the door and sees his wife's face, he instantly remembers that he was supposed to get milk. The wife is angry and says, "I asked you to do one simple thing! Was it really that difficult to get milk?!" And the argument begins.

The husband drives home from work every day and never has to get milk. On that fateful day, he followed his well-established pattern of coming home and went right past the store.

It's not the case that the husband doesn't care about his wife or didn't listen to her request. He fully intended to get the milk. The problem is he didn't create a tool for prompting him to do something different on the way home, like an alarm on his cell phone or a Post-It Note on his steering wheel.

The husband can apologize and go get the milk immediately. That would be living up to his responsibility. The wife can step back and see that the husband's intent wasn't malicious; his actions were understandable.

Each of them can resolve the situation easily with emotional intelligence: understanding their emotions in themselves and the other person.

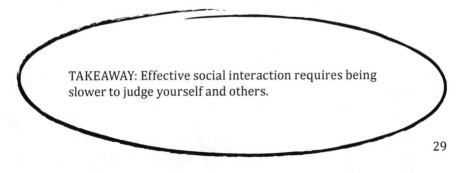

TAKEAWAY: Effective social interaction requires being slower to judge yourself and others.

Lesson 9
Pillar 4: Relationship Management

To say my fate is not tied to your fate is like saying, "Your end of the boat is sinking."

~ Hugh Downs

People won't remember what you said. People won't remember what you did. But people will always remember how you made them feel.

~ Maya Angelou

By this point, it should be fairly easy to see how the first three pillars of EI — self-awareness, self-management, and social awareness — feed directly into relationship management.

When you have great relationships — when you figure out how to manage your relationships — you create a more complete life. One might say that learning to develop great relationships is a major part of what life is about.

At this stage, you can ask yourself some key questions:

What shape are my relationships in? What is my role or responsibility for the state of those relationships? Do I hold grudges and blame others easily so I don't have to face the possibility that I myself am at fault? Do I push people away because I'm afraid they might find out who I really am and they won't like me?

I had a friend who was married five times before she was 35 years old. She finally understood that she was the only common denominator in all of those relationships. Her relationship management was terrible.

She came to understand that she needed to return to self-awareness and self-management before her relationships would improve. Through a lot of hard work, she realized that, for so many years, she pushed men away before they could hurt her. She protected herself as much as possible to avoid getting taken advantage of, abandoned, left.

After doing the work on herself, she married for the sixth time. She's now been married for more than 30 years.

Relationships are about connection, engagement, and collaboration. They are a source of your real power. It's great to be self-aware, but that's only the first step. Emotional intelligence is about understanding your own emotions, those of other people, *and* using that information to develop your relationships effectively.

When you're locked down in protecting yourself and interact with anger, impatience, and nastiness as a habit, this really says more about you than the people you're dealing with.

Am I hostile at work? Do I have a reputation as a difficult person? Am I stressed out all the time and snap at people? Do I pout and whine when I don't get what I want or defensive when someone looks at me the wrong way?

These may be indications that you're still in reaction mode, and perhaps even reacting to things that have nothing to do with the person you're in relationship with. Do you see how things from the past may be informing your present relationships?

One type of person I meet a lot is the one who says, "I don't sugarcoat things. If they don't like what I have to say, tough. They're going to get the unvarnished truth out of me."

The fact is few people can stand to hear the unvarnished truth, even (maybe especially) the person who never sugarcoats anything. You can't expect to steamroll over everybody and have great relationships.

We are emotional beings first and foremost, and the best way to get the best out of other people is to respect them.

TAKEAWAY: Your ability to relate to and interact with other people is a source of your power and influence.

Lesson 10

Pulling Pins and Throwing Grenades

*No one can make you feel inferior
without your consent.*

~ Eleanor Roosevelt

*Isolated people have a vastly increased rate of
premature death from all causes and
are 3-5 times likelier to die early than
people with strong social ties.*

~ Dean Ornish

One day, almost 20 years ago, I was at my mother's house working at her dining room table on my laptop.

My 10-year-old niece asked if she could play video games on it. I said, "Yes, but..." Be careful. Don't press the buttons too hard. Get that soda away from it. Everything to convey the message, "Don't you dare break it!"

My younger sister was in the room and she said, "What are you doing?!" "What?!" I replied. "Just let her use the laptop!" I was quickly becoming indignant. "That's my laptop! I have a lot of important things on it!" And we were off to the races.

In the next couple of minutes, we re-enacted behavior we'd seen countless times growing up, mostly from my father. He was a charming, talented, and bright man who could have a temper that would scare even the hardiest of souls.

He had a special talent for latching on to the most innocuous comments made by someone, often at the dinner table, and reacting to them.

Then, he'd draw in everything that had been bothering him for the past weeks or months, as if reminded he hadn't exploded about those things yet. He would get up from the table and yell.

He'd move halfway down the table and yell. He'd get to the end of the table and yell.

Next, he'd retreat into the family room, grab the remote, and put up the newspaper. Conversation over.

He modeled the way to handle conflict. I thought of the process as pulling pins, throwing grenades, and getting the hell out of there.

And that's what happened that day with my sister in my mother's dining room. We pulled our pins and threw our grenades at each other.

Up to that point, we really didn't have any other language to express our feelings. We didn't so much as resolve conflict as steamroll over it and bury it. We could play at forgetting things ever happened.

It was simply one of the countless ways we brought unresolved childhood thoughts and behaviors into adulthood.

My sister and I were up in each other's faces, pulling pins and throwing grenades, and then I turned to leave. That is, after all, the next step in the dance. That's what I watched my father do.

I turned to leave, took one step, and froze in my tracks.

Unexpectedly to me and her, I turned back and said, "Why do we do this? This never gets us anywhere." Instantly, her body relaxed and the tension disappeared from her shoulders. That was a major moment for me in which I consciously changed my relationship management.

TAKEAWAY: Your ability to change from reacting to responding will improve your relationships.

Lesson 11
Components of Emotional Intelligence

An emotion occurs when there are certain biological, certain experiential, and certain cognitive states which all occur simultaneously.

~ John D. Mayer

Emotional intelligence is not the opposite of intelligence, it is not the triumph of heart over head — it is the unique intersection of both.

~ David Caruso

We can break down emotional intelligence into three main components. The important part here is to remember that all three are interconnected and in constant interaction with each other. What happens with one component influences the others, which, in turn, loop back to influence the original component and each other.

Cognitive

Cognition is simply the mental action or process of acquiring knowledge and understanding through thought, experiences, and the senses. Your thoughts, beliefs, and perceptions determine how you see the world.

The way you interpret the world is influenced by the thoughts you have as a result of your upbringing, environment, books you've read, conversations you've had, and so on. We all get to create our own reality regardless of the events that are actually happening around us. More on this later.

What kind of emotional intelligence do you suppose you would have if everything you experienced came through a lens of anger, sadness, pessimism, negativity, cynicism, and hopelessness?

Behavioral

The thoughts that are coursing through your brain are then influencing how you will behave. If you believe that everything in the world outside your house is dangerous, you may choose to stay in all day and never go out.

If you grew up watching the news constantly, you might think there's danger at every turn. If you had pessimistic parents who didn't trust anyone, you might have adopted their perspective and come to the conclusion that no one can be trusted and, therefore, you don't go to parties, go on dates, have deep relationships, or you choose to run away when people try to get close.

Physical

The third component is physical. As you doubtless already know, the first two components are going to influence your physical state. Your negative emotional state may produce headaches, stomach aches, insomnia, and other physical manifestations.

You may respond to your own thoughts or behaviors with binge eating or drinking, a steady diet of junk food, or bad sleep habits.

The physical will then loop back to impact the cognitive and behavioral. The worse you feel physically, the worse you are likely to think about yourself, which may make you impatient, intolerant, or generally belligerent in your behavior toward other people.

Likewise, your positive emotional state may produce confidence, optimism, and hopefulness. This will likely result in more healthy interactions with people and open the door to opportunity and possibility that you would not have access to as a negative person.

TAKEAWAY: The three components are constantly interacting with each other, governed largely by your emotional intelligence.

Lesson 12
What People with High EI Do

*Maturity is achieved when a person
postpones immediate pleasures for long-term values.*
~ Joshua L. Liebman

*Emotional intelligence is the distinguishing factor
that determines if we make lemonade when life
hands us lemons or spend our life stuck in bitterness.*
~ Adele B. Lynn

So often we can read books and hear lectures about emotional intelligence but not have any idea of steps to take in real life.

The following is a list of things that people high in EI do on a regular basis. Some of these things are actions, some are simply ways of being.

You may be the kind of person who makes everything more difficult than it needs to be. Life is hard enough. You don't need to stack the deck against yourself. So here's the bottom line: emotional intelligence is not rocket science. The most important thing to do is get out of your own way.

Focus on present and near future. The past is gone and although you may need to reinterpret it, you don't want to get stuck there. Likewise, don't get overwhelmed by the far-off future, worrying about things that might or might not happen. Decide what you want, make a plan, get to work.

Get out of comfort zone. Outside the comfort zone can be scary, but it's also where growth, experience, courage, risk, and a lot of other important things take place to move you forward. Staying in your comfort zone is to stagnate and to stagnate is to die.

Listen to the right people. So many people around you are giving you advice about how you should live your life. Look beyond their words and see if they themselves have practiced what they're preaching. Be discerning about who you take advice from. Disregard those who are talking just to talk. If you want to become a millionaire, don't ask your broke uncle for advice.

Expect change and prepare for it. You may be afraid of change, but change is one of the few things you can count on. The Greek philosophers said the only constant in life is change. You get to choose whether you're going to bury yourself in your old ways or embrace the future. Yes, it may be unknown and even scary, but the alternative is to reject who you might become.

Stay open-minded. People high in EI know they don't know everything. Even things they think they know remain open for reinterpretation when new information becomes available. They know the world is complex with a multitude of perspectives. Solutions to problems often come from the most unlikely places and an open mind has a better chance of seeing them.

Celebrate other people's success. If you're jealous of someone's success and try to undermine it, dismiss it, or try to one-up them, that's a good indication of your own insecurity. Your EI isn't as high as it could be. High EI means supporting and encouraging others in their journeys. Exploring your self-awareness helps you understand why you might be motivated to downplay others' success.

Take responsibility. People high in EI don't wallow in self-pity or blame others for the way their life is turning out. In the face of defeat or dissatisfaction, they take responsibility for their own lives and get to work to improve what they can. They understand that no one is coming with a magic wand or the winning lottery ticket to make everything right in their lives.

As you can see, this isn't rocket science. But it does require that you get inside the four pillars of EI to see how good you are at doing the things that people high in EI do.

TAKEAWAY: Do what people high in EI do in order to improve your own EI.

Lesson 13
Do You Need to Improve Your EI?

The measure of intelligence is the ability to change.
~ Albert Einstein

There is only one corner of the universe you can be certain of improving...and that's your own self.
~ Aldous Huxley

You may not be sure of the state of your emotional intelligence. You can become more familiar with yours by considering the following statements. If they apply to you, your EI may be in need of an overhaul.

- You often feel like others don't get the point and it makes you impatient and frustrated.
- You're surprised when others are sensitive to your comments or jokes and you think they're overreacting.
- You think being liked at work is overrated.
- You weigh in early with your assertions and defend them with rigor.
- You find others are to blame for most of the issues on your team.
- You find it annoying when others expect you to know how they feel.

Professor Chi-Sum Wong and Professor Kenneth Law developed the following emotional intelligence inventory that can help you further understand your emotional intelligence.

Understand and express your own emotions. People with this ability know how they're feeling before other people do.

1. I have a good sense of why I have certain feelings most of the time.
2. I have a good understanding of my own emotions.
3. I really understand what I feel.
4. I always know whether or not I am happy.

Perceive and understand the emotions of others around you. This ability means that you are sensitive to how others are feeling.

5. I always know my friends' emotions from their behavior.
6. I am a good observer of others' emotions.
7. I am sensitive to the feelings and emotions of others.
8. I have a good understanding of the emotions of people around me.

Regulate your own emotion. Regulating your emotions means that you are able to keep them under control, especially when you're feeling distressed.

9. I always set goals for myself and then try my best to achieve them.
10. I always tell myself I am a competent person.
11. I am a self-motivated person.
12. I would always encourage myself to try my best.

Use emotion to maximize performance. Directing your emotions toward constructive activities allows you to use them to use them to optimal advantage.

13. I am able to control my temper and handle difficulties rationally.
14. I am quite capable of controlling my own emotions.
15. I can always calm down quickly when I am very angry.
16. I have good control of my own emotions.

Take time to reflect on how these statements apply to your life.

TAKEAWAY: Face the brutal facts about your emotional intelligence to improve your life.

Part 2

Fear and EI

Lesson 14

Fear

Avoidance is the disease. Non-avoidance is the cure.
                                                            ~ Unknown

Fears are educated into us, and can, if we wish, be educated out.
                                         ~ Karl Menninger

If we're going to dig into emotional intelligence, we have to talk a bit about fear.

Consider this: If you let go of an object, it will drop to the floor. If you drop the object ten times, it will drop to the floor each of those ten times.

Nothing in the way you drop the object, nothing in the way you think about the way it falls, will change the fact that it falls. It's a physical law. We can't change gravity.

But most issues pertaining to fear are not scientific in the same way gravity is. You can change the way you think about fear. Later, I'll talk about the role of brain function in emotional intelligence, but for the moment, I'm interested in the stories you have told yourself and the possibility of changing them.

In this lesson, I want to bring to the front of your mind the idea that, outside of physical laws, by and large we created the world around us. And if we made it up, we can change it.

For example, concepts like time, age, and money are constructs — we gave them their meaning so that we as human beings could orient ourselves in a certain way to reduce the chaos around us.

You can choose to look at time, age, and money any way you'd like. A person who is sixty-eight can feel like he's ninety, and someone who is eighty-six can feel like she's seventeen. Some see the opportunity in five spare minutes; others think it's too short to do anything.

When you were born, decisions were made for you and most every major aspect of your life was determined by someone else. By and large, the country you grew up in, the members of your family, your religion, your social circles, your education, and so much more were someone else's doing. Your beliefs — and, in turn, many of your fears — are concepts that were influenced by those factors and others.

The belief systems of others and your interpretations of them created and influenced your own belief system, your psychology, your perceptions, your decision-making process, your choices, and your fears. This will be an important consideration in our further discussion of emotional intelligence.

So, there are a couple of important points for you to bring to the front of your mind at the outset of your journey:

First, certain choices were made for you by others on the grounds that you were helpless to make those choices yourself. You didn't decide where you lived, where you went to school, or what religious beliefs you followed.

Second, much of your fear comes from your own imperfect interpretations of the messages you received in your environment at a young age. You couldn't imagine that something else was really bothering Mom when she exploded at you; it must have been your fault.

Third, conditions change — you grow up — giving you the opportunity and perhaps the responsibility to reinterpret what you received from others in order to become your own true self. That is, to develop self-awareness and social awareness.

In part, fear (showing itself as guilt, worry, anxiety, stress, and others) is born of that struggle between continuing to hold on to and live up to the ideals that were imprinted on you in your childhood and re-creating yourself into a new, independent, and self-aware individual.

TAKEAWAY: You get to choose every day who you are.

Lesson 15

The Fear List

*The greatest mistake a man can make
is to be afraid of making one.*
~ Elbert Hubbard

*Failure is an inescapable part of life and
a critically important part of any successful life.*
~ Tal Ben-Shahar

Ask others what they are afraid of, and frequently the initial responses you get include spiders, snakes, heights, and the dentist.

Probe a little deeper and the list of fears becomes more delicate, more sensitive, and more profound. Facial expressions change to reveal the existence of more intimate secrets. Their faces become childlike, as if they're being transported to an earlier moment in time when those fears were initially experienced.

At the same time, they look weary from hanging on to those fears for a very long time.

More than anything, as we ask more people, the list becomes predictable and very familiar.

- Fear of making mistakes
- Fear of rejection
- Fear of embarrassment
- Fear of criticism

- Fear of losing approval/love

- Fear of losing control

- Fear of failure

- Fear of success

At first glance, you may feel your stomach tightening and your palms getting sweaty just thinking about what triggers fear in you: stress at work, arguments with loved ones, public speaking, writing a book, never-ending responsibility, living up to expectations, and more. We all experience some of these fears at one time or other.

One of the most critical exercises to do throughout your life is to make clear for yourself the distinction between true fear and false fear and how each may play a role in your life.

Dr. Lissa Rankin, author of *The Fear Cure*, says true fear is generated when there is, in fact, a threat to one's being in the moment as it is happening.

False fear is driven by the *anticipation* of something going wrong, being bad, or happening. So often, you stop yourself from trying new things because of the *possibility* of negative consequences, because of the thought of *potential* discomfort.

Losing control of your car or being followed by someone on a dark street generates true fear. The *thought* of possibly losing control of your car or being followed by someone on a dark street is false fear.

So many of the thoughts you have are leading you to false fears that show up as stress and anxiety. This, in turn, lowers your emotional intelligence and your ability to effectively interact with others.

TAKEAWAY: Increasing your awareness of your fear will help improve your emotional intelligence.

Lesson 16
Fear of Public Speaking

*I failed public speaking in grade school
'cause I was so nervous and scared.*

~ Gary Clark, Jr.

*Fear paralyzes you — fear of flying, fear of the future,
fear of leaving a rubbish marriage, fear of public
speaking, or whatever it is.*

~ Annie Lennox

There is such a variety and multitude of false fears you generate that the examples are endless. One that you might relate to is the fear of public speaking. And, indeed, it was a major fear of mine.

When I was in high school, we had assignments to recite poems in front of class. I would spend hours worrying about the prospect of standing before my classmates and performing.

On the big day, I would face my peers. I would look into the audience and start to create stories in my mind — stories about what they were thinking. I would take all of my fears and project them on to my classmates.

What if they don't like my performance? What if I forget the next line? What if I use the wrong inflection? What if I get a failing grade? What if I'm the worst out of all of the students?

I would quickly convince myself that my classmates didn't like my recitation, that they were bored with me, that they thought I was terrible. Blood would rush to my head and fill my ears. I felt like I was in a cloud of cotton.

I couldn't think straight; all of my thoughts jumbled in my head. I would forget the next line and stumble my way through the assignment. And not even all the way to the end of the assignment, because I never actually finished.

The teacher would approach with an attitude like, "Poor, pathetic Joe. We know you can't do this. Have a seat."

The thing about this fear is that it all happened inside my head. There was no real threat to me, only false fear generated by my thoughts. I was never in any danger; my physical well-being was never at risk. It was mainly my ego that would suffer.

My fear of public speaking was so strong and I was so locked down to the idea of being able to do it, I created the conditions in which I virtually ensured my failure.

The false fear showed up as questions I asked myself in a panic: What if I make a mistake? What if I feel embarrassed? What if my classmates laugh at me? What if I'm not accepted and not acceptable? What if I'm a failure?

I would come to realize that all of these false fears were symptoms of deeper things, things that kept me from being my true self, fears that kept me paralyzed from moving forward.

I would come to realize that all of these false fears were directly related to my emotional intelligence. Only when I started to deconstruct these fears through self-awareness and self-management could I change the way I thought and change the actions I took.

With public speaking, I realized that people in the audience were more afraid than I was. I realized that worrying about what they thought was one of the reasons I failed. I realized that my fear was merely a symptom of the general sense of negativity, pessimism, and hopelessness I had generated as a child.

> TAKEAWAY: False fear may be keeping you from exploring the four pillars of emotional intelligence.

Lesson 17
Expectations and Reality

The best things in life are unexpected, because there were no expectations.

~ Eli Khamarov

The outer conditions of a person's life will always be found to reflect their inner beliefs.

~ James Allen

What is it you believe about yourself and the world around you?

I've mentioned this before and it will be a major theme throughout the book. A lot of what you choose to do in your life comes down to what is, what you think should be, and how large the gap is between those two things.

Fear often generates the gap between your expectations about yourself and your beliefs of others' expectations for you, on the one hand, and "reality," on the other hand. And, in turn, even more fear is generated as the gap expands.

What happens in your life is frequently determined by how large that gap between expectations and reality becomes and, more importantly, what you choose to fill that gap with.

For example, if there's very little gap between expectations and reality, you likely have done a lot of work on the four pillars of emotional intelligence. You likely have identified your major fears, understood that they're primarily inside your head, and that you're the only one who can take responsibility for them.

You have observed the world and determined what works for you, what makes sense to you, and what deserves a response and what doesn't. You have sized up people and situations by listening and looking. You have reduced your need to control everything and everyone around you.

The gap between expectations and reality gets larger when you feel like you have to satisfy the needs of other people, live up to the opinions and judgments of other people, be acceptable in the eyes of other people. Of course, sometimes it's important to do those things, but not to the point where the gap gets too large.

When the gap gets larger, you buy expensive cars and clothing to feel better about yourself or to create a specific perception for the outside world about your level of success.

When the gap gets larger, you feel the need to control and manipulate people so that they fit into your expectation of what reality should look like.

When the gap gets larger, you spend hours in front of the television, eat compulsively, and indulge in other low-level addictions, feeling that you can't bridge the gap between expectations and reality.

When the gap gets larger, you get depressed, drink too much, abuse drugs, and inflict pain on others. Your frustration has increased to such a level that you don't know how to handle it anymore. In many cases, you've decided that you can't handle it.

The gap can begin to get away from you if you don't slow down long enough to understand your expectations and the reality surrounding you.

Are you demanding that everyone's reality conforms to your expectations?

Are you guilt-ridden or beating yourself up because the reality you're living doesn't conform to the expectations of your parents, church, community, or peers?

Do you have expectations for yourself that are unreasonable and maybe even unreachable?

TAKEAWAY: The larger the gap between expectations and reality, the harder it is to maintain good emotional intelligence.

Lesson 18

Handling Fear

We fear something before we hate it; a child who fears noises becomes a man who hates noises.
~ Cyril Connolly

How we relate to fear determines how we do in life, and maybe it is the essence of who we are.
~ Thom Rutledge

What is your fear saying to you? If you look at the list of fears in Lesson 15, you could summarize it as "I can't handle it."

- I can't handle the possibility of being embarrassed.
- I can't handle the possibility of being criticized.
- I can't handle the possibility of being rejected.
- I can't handle the possibility of failing.

Your response to this mantra of "I can't handle" frequently is to give mediocre or unsuccessful performances, like me trying to recite poems in high school. Other times, you simply don't try, preferring to stay in the safety of your comfort zone.

If you try and fail, you can say, "See, I knew this wouldn't work."

If you avoid it altogether, you can save yourself from pain. After all, that's what we as human beings try to do: minimize pain and enhance pleasure.

But the more you think about failing, the more you talk about how difficult something will be, the more you complain about the task at hand, the greater the likelihood you will see your fears come into being. *That which you focus on expands.*

You're too busy protecting yourself from false fear, treating it as if it's true fear.

And it doesn't require a sudden, dramatic event in your life to make you believe you can't handle it. It's already happened, slowly, subtly. You created the responses a long time ago to the events you think you're afraid of now.

You play these responses over and over again in your head.

The protective layers built up over the years have pushed the walls of your comfort zone in closer and closer to the point where you don't want to risk very much or take too many chances, if any. In many cases, those walls have become so thick that breaking through them can be difficult.

Emotional intelligence provides a road map for facing your fears by questioning whether they're true or false. With greater self-awareness and self-management, you can strip away the stories you've told yourself, decrease the gap between expectations and reality, and change your stance about your relationships and your life from passive to proactive.

Facing fear means starting to understand you can handle much more than you believe you can.

Facing fear means crafting for yourself a new story about your past, to change your beliefs, your assumptions, and your responses.

Facing fear means improving your emotional intelligence.

You deal with fear not by dancing around it or eliminating it, but by going through it — having courage to act not in the absence of fear but in spite of it. You won't do it unless you have a plan with good tools and techniques to improve your life.

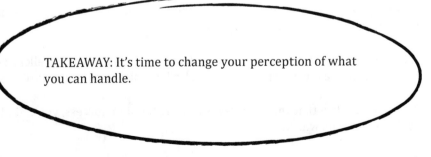

TAKEAWAY: It's time to change your perception of what you can handle.

Lesson 19

Moving Forward

The best way out is always through.
　　　　　　　　　　　~ Helen Keller

*Love is what we were born with.
Fear is what we learned here.*
　　　　　　　　　~ Marianne Williamson

In your mind's eye, you can sometimes look at the big picture, the daunting totality of what you're trying to accomplish, and bury yourself in fear. You allow the fear to dictate how you proceed.

So often you later find that your initial fears were unwarranted. Before long, you get past the fear and address the task at hand. When you pushed fear to the side, you accomplished the task much quicker than anticipated.

As always, you have a choice.

You can allow fear to prevent you from doing things you dream about or you can find a way to manage your fear and move forward into things you never dreamed possible.

When you realize that everyone — even the most successful among us — has fear, you'll find it easier to move forward.

When you realize that perfectionism — not to be confused with excellence — has no role in the creative process, you'll find it easier to move forward.

When you realize that the universe is rooting for your success, you'll find it easier to move forward.

When you realize that all creativity — life itself — is about taking small steps on a daily basis, here and now, toward improved emotional intelligence, you'll find it easier to move forward.

It is useful to reframe how you think about fear. It doesn't take advanced degrees or special talent.

Self-awareness and effective tools and techniques introduced into your daily life will help dramatically reduce the impact of fear and improve your emotional intelligence.

Here are useful ways to reframe your thoughts about fear:

- Understand the difference between your true fear and false fear.
- Realize that fear can be a result of interpretations of events from childhood, a time when you weren't qualified to accurately interpret what was actually happening around you.
- Resist the urge to compare how you feel on the inside to how others look on the outside. It may appear that others are fearless. They're not.
- Create mechanisms, games, and psychological tricks to counteract the fear that creeps up inside you.
- Develop the habit of preparing well for whatever you set out to do. Proper preparation prevents poor performance — and goes a long way to reduce fear.
- Don't try to complicate or overthink your task. Just the opposite — KISS: Keep It Super Simple.
- Understand that perfectionism and procrastination are traps keeping you from living your life.
- Do your best to serve others. When you serve, you can enhance your appreciation for what you have and improve your empathy for others. You put your fear in perspective when you get out of your own head and engage with others.

TAKEAWAY: Managing your fear and moving forward is a key part of improving your emotional intelligence.

Part 3

Inside Your Brain

Lesson 20
Reptilian Brain

Habit is stronger than reason.
> ~ Santayana

Brain: an apparatus with which we think we think.
> ~ Ambrose Bierce

When you hear the words "emotional intelligence," you may think primarily about emotions. And, of course, emotions are central.

You may, however, overlook the role of the brain when trying to change how you respond to your emotions. Understanding even a little about the brain can help you improve your emotional intelligence dramatically and quickly.

After taking a brief tour of brain function in the next several lessons, I'll tie it to effective tools and techniques that you can use to improve your cognitive, behavioral, and physical responses to situations around you.

The first part of the brain worth mentioning is the so-called reptilian brain, the oldest and most primitive part.

It's made up of the cerebellum, the basal ganglia, and the upper part of the spinal cord.

The reptilian brain generally controls basic vital body functions such as heart rate, breathing, body temperature, and balance. It's thought to represent the core of the nervous system.

It also controls voluntary movements and routine or "habitual" behaviors such as eye movements, cognition, and emotions.

The reptilian brain is involved in determining which of several possible behaviors to execute at any given time. This is referred to as "behavior switching" and is influenced by signals from many parts of the brain, including the prefrontal cortex. In the next few lessons you'll see why this is important to keep in mind.

In earliest childhood, one's mental state is controlled almost completely by the reptilian brain.

When children are vying for attention or trying to stake out their own territory and creating their own identity, the reptilian brain is largely at work.

Compulsive reactions like attraction and aggression start in the reptilian brain.

Basic instincts like the drive for physical dominance or trying to establish and defend territory are driven by the reptilian brain.

The reptilian brain controls or influences behaviors driven by basic survival, social interaction, sexual interaction, and territoriality. These are instinctive and our responses are automatic.

It may not be too surprising to find the following behaviors coming out of the reptilian brain:

- Obsessive-compulsive behavior
- Daily rituals and superstitious acts
- Conformance to old ways of doing things
- Ceremonial re-enactments
- Obeying or observing precedent in legal, religious, cultural, and other matters
- Deception

You can find many of these behaviors and activities in daily life today, helping you understand the terrain you're operating in, acquire and control territory, protect yourself, build social structures, and survive.

TAKEAWAY: Activities of the reptilian brain are fundamental to your survival.

Lesson 21

The Amygdala

*Bad news sells because the amygdala
is always looking for something to fear.*

~ Peter Diamandis

*Pain is what the world inflicts upon us. Suffering is
our emotional reaction when we fail to make the
difficult conscious choice to choose Joy.*

~ Jonathan Lockwood Huie

The limbic system, the second part of the brain, is made up of a number of parts including the amygdala, hippocampus, thalamus, and hypothalamus. It supports a variety of functions including emotion, behavior, motivation, long-term memory, and the sense of smell.

For purposes of our discussion, the amygdala will be the center of attention.

The amygdala is a small but powerful part of the limbic system that's crucial for survival. It continually scans your environment for danger, interpreting whether you're safe or at risk. (There are actually two, one in each hemisphere of the brain, collectively called the amygdalae.)

The amygdala reacts extremely quickly, which is part of its strength as well as its weakness.

If it didn't act quickly enough, chances are the human race would have been extinguished long ago.

On the down side, the amygdala reacts so fast that it often doesn't have all of the information surrounding a situation before triggering an emotional reaction.

When the limbic system is activated and the stress hormones secreted, all of the bodily functions shift to focus on one result: survival.

The problem is, survival today means something very different from the original challenges that faced the limbic system. The most important thing back then was to stay alive when facing everyday threats like predators.

Today, the same mechanism gets activated when you feel threatened in any way. The same hormones get secreted and the fight, flight, or freeze instinct turns on. Unfortunately, the threat could be that someone looked at you the wrong way, cut you off on the highway, or disrespected you. And you tend to stay in that mode for hours, days, or weeks whereas your ancestors would shut it off once their survival was ensured.

Imagine if the amygdala and the limbic system get activated during a conversation that simply made you feel uncomfortable. The same powerful hormones (like cortisol and adrenaline) that your ancestors needed to survive a saber-tooth tiger threat are secreted.

Remember Vinnie, the detective who had a problem with his temper? His fundamental problem was that he was being taken over by his amygdala and he didn't know how to handle it.

The amygdala assesses both external and internal information for threats and emotional importance; that is, it works on events outside yourself, like experiences and traumas, as well as internal processes, like thoughts and beliefs.

A critical thing to realize is that the amygdala can learn to reduce its reaction to stimuli. Understanding this and learning the tools and techniques for doing it is a major driver behind high emotional intelligence.

It's difficult to overestimate the importance of the amygdala in understanding your emotions, those of others, and changing your reactions into responses in any given situation.

TAKEAWAY: The amygdala plays a central role in triggering your emotional responses.

Lesson 22
The Prefrontal Cortex

*Experience is not what happens to you —
it's how you interpret what happens to you.*

~ Aldous Huxley

*The sign of intelligent people is their ability to
control emotions by the application of reason.*

~ Marya Mannes

The prefrontal cortex is known as "the brain's good boss," guiding you when you're at your best.

Known as the third brain — after the reptilian brain and the limbic system — the prefrontal cortex is the newest, most recently developed part of the brain in the evolutionary timetable.

The prefrontal cortex is responsible for a number of functions critical to high emotional intelligence, such as:

- Solving personal and interpersonal problems
- Managing impulses
- Expressing feelings effectively
- Relating well to others
- Facilitating rational thought and decision making

The most commonly used term for functions carried out by the prefrontal cortex is executive function.

Executive function relates to your ability to differentiate among conflicting thoughts, determine good and bad, better and best, same and different, and future consequences of current activities.

Executive function also includes working toward a defined goal, predicting outcomes, developing expectations based on actions, and controlling socially unacceptable urges.

In a nutshell, the prefrontal cortex's basic activity is coordinating thoughts and actions with internal goals.

As you could imagine, the prefrontal cortex is an important player in your ability to prevent or bounce back from emotional traumas.

Located behind the forehead, the prefrontal cortex is the last part of the brain to develop in each individual as development proceeds from the back of the brain to the front; it isn't until one's early to mid-20s that the prefrontal cortex becomes fully developed.

This late growth and development is likely the reason some otherwise intelligent and sensible teens engage in high-risk or excessive behaviors even though they may understand the potential dangers.

Have you ever stood back and scratched your head in wonder at how that teenager could possibly be your offspring?

One of the major explanations is that the prefrontal cortex is incapable of responding quickly enough to counter the extremely fast emotional reactions of the limbic system and the reptilian brain.

The prefrontal cortex provides a greater range of responses than other parts of the brain when presented with stimuli, information, or an event. But it has to be activated.

TAKEAWAY: The prefrontal cortex governs executive function and helps counteract the emotion of the limbic system and reptilian brain.

Lesson 23
The Amygdala and Prefrontal Cortex Battle

*We're emotional beings so our first response
will always be emotional.*

~ Travis Bradberry

*The emotional brain responds to an event
more quickly than the thinking brain.*

~ Daniel Goleman

The struggle between the amygdala and the prefrontal cortex is one of the key themes in emotional intelligence.

And one of the keys in improving emotional intelligence is to be aware of, understand, and intervene in this struggle to ensure good outcomes.

For that reason, it's critical to build effective techniques to short-circuit the dramatic emotional reaction of the amygdala and give yourself a chance to fully process the information you're receiving through the prefrontal cortex. Everything depends on it.

As you have noticed in the past two lessons, the prefrontal cortex and the amygdala can be odds with each other in some ways. The prefrontal cortex is related more toward rational thinking and executive decision making; the amygdala leans heavily toward emotion.

The amygdala reacts very quickly — 80,000 times faster than the prefrontal cortex — which creates a challenge. Generally speaking, nerve signals go through the limbic system before reaching the prefrontal cortex.

The amygdala reacts and can be out of control before the rational, executive decision making function of the prefrontal cortex can kick in.

A consequence of reacting very quickly is that the amygdala misses a lot of information. You may often jump into a conflict without having enough information about what's really going on.

On top of that, the amygdala and prefrontal cortex are sending signals back and forth to each other, but the amygdala sends far more toward the prefrontal cortex than the prefrontal cortex sends to the amygdala.

All of that means that it's easy to react to internal and external information in an emotional way. If you get stuck in the emotion of the moment without allowing the signals to go on to your prefrontal cortex, you are likely to experience an amygdala hijack.

During an amygdala hijack, you'll essentially be incapable of responding to the situation in a rational, calm way. Your emotions will take over and you'll be far less able to control your thoughts, words, or actions.

Remember what I did on the boat in China? It was an emotional response which I arrived at before letting my prefrontal cortex get involved.

I was essentially blinded by emotion — the emotion of not being able to control the situation, compounded by the emotion I was reliving from childhood.

When you regularly remind yourself that your emotional life has a neurological basis, affecting your hormones and your ability to respond to events that happen around you, it becomes easier to control your responses.

When you increase your self-awareness and self-management, begin to answer the three cornerstone questions (Who am I? What do I want? How am I going to get it?), understand your triggers, and use the pause button actively to regulate your brain signals like Vinnie did, you'll begin to dramatically improve your emotional intelligence.

The rest of the book will provide numerous ways to do this.

TAKEAWAY: Understanding and regulating the struggle between the prefrontal cortex and the amygdala is central to your emotional success.

Lesson 24

Fight, Flight, Freeze... or a Different Way

Adopting the right attitude can convert a negative stress into a positive one.

~ Hans Selye

Slow down and everything you are chasing will come around and catch you.

~ John De Paola

Imagine it's 10,000 B.C. and you're leading your tribe through treacherous terrain, constantly scanning the horizon for threats, all senses alert to the possibility of danger.

Suddenly, a saber-toothed tiger leaps from behind a rock and takes chase.

In an instant, your pituitary gland signals the adrenal glands to flood your bloodstream with stress hormones, including adrenaline, aldosterone, and cortisol.

Your heart rate increases, you hyperventilate, more oxygen flows throughout your body, and your senses heighten further as blood is directed away from digestion and other non-essential functions. Your immune system is suppressed to free up resources.

You stick around to engage the threat since you can now think more quickly, perform with greater strength, and feel less pain. Fight.

Or, you decide to make a run for it to safety, on legs that move faster and with a brain that thinks more quickly under the influence of the activated stress hormones. Flight.

Or, you don't know what to do. Your brain shuts down, confusion reigns, and you're simply scared into paralysis. Freeze.

After the event passes (and you're not dead), your body's systems return to normal. Levels of adrenaline and cortisol in your bloodstream decrease, causing your heart rate to lower, blood pressure to drop, and all other functions of the body to come back online.

The problem with all of this is that you don't have to fight saber-tooted tigers these days and yet you use exactly the same fight, flight, or freeze reactions to deal with non-life-threatening situations.

You may not even realize that, over time, you've gotten to the point of not being able to turn off your fight-flight-freeze response mechanism. Being in constant fight-flight-freeze mode impacts your communication, focus, nutrition, and general health. It undermines your performance and productivity. You get less sleep, drink more caffeine, and eventually feel rundown.

The different way, the way to dramatically reduce the intensity of fight-flight-freeze, is to develop high emotional intelligence.

Vinnie the police detective was constantly in fight mode when what he really wanted was peace, tranquility, and a great family life. He didn't know about the struggle going on between his amygdala and prefrontal cortex. He had no way to regulate that battle.

My father was constantly in fight-flight mode. He would pick a one-sided fight, explode, and then flee the scene. In this way, he could maintain dominance and control without questioning what was happening inside him. During his fight-flight outbursts, most of us in the house fell into freeze mode.

Emotional intelligence helps you to face yourself, understand what you truly want, and how to improve your chances of getting it.

TAKEAWAY: Emotional intelligence helps you regulate the extremes of fight, flight, or freeze so that you can make better responses.

Part 4

Making the Right Choices

Lesson 25
The Chinese Farmer

All that we are is the result of what we have thought.
> ~ Buddha

*If you can't change the circumstances,
change your perspective.*
> ~ Unknown

At the core of emotional intelligence is your sense of self-awareness. Every day you choose who you are going to be that day. Your self-management drives the decisions you make when faced with choices. I've found the following story from Steve Hagen's book, *Buddhism: Plain and Simple*, a good reminder of this.

One day, the only horse of a Chinese farmer runs away. The farmer's neighbor runs over and exclaims, "How terrible! Your horse ran away!" The farmer responds, "Who knows what's good or bad?"

The next day the horse returns with 50 other horses trailing. The neighbor runs over and exclaims, "How wonderful! You have 50 new horses!" The farmer responds, "Who knows what's good or bad?"

While breaking in one of the new horses, the farmer's son is thrown and breaks his leg. The neighbor runs over and exclaims, "How terrible! Your son broke his leg!" The farmer responds, "Who knows what's good or bad?"

The next day the Chinese military comes through the town conscripting all the young males but not the farmer's son because of his broken leg. The neighbor runs over and exclaims, "How wonderful! They didn't take your son!" The farmer responds, "Who knows what's good or bad?"

Where does this story end? If you're the neighbor, it never does. If you're the farmer, it just is what it is.

But don't misunderstand. "It is what it is" is not resignation to the situation. It means that you have come face to face with a situation — now, what good can you bring about from it?

If you're like the neighbor, you will be shifting with the wind every time it changes direction. You'll find yourself on an emotional rollercoaster, responding to the superficial nature of events.

The farmer understands the nature of the universe and the nature of the human condition. The farmer understands emotional intelligence.

You very well may be creating your own stress, your own insecurity, your own fear, through your interpretations of what happens around you.

Whether you *react* or *respond* to stress, insecurity, and fear will tell you a lot about how you will proceed after that.

If you convince yourself that the stress, insecurity, and fear you feel is "bad," your reactions to that stress will tend to be negative and judgmental. It may result in procrastination, excuses, and blaming. Your amygdala will take over.

If you decide stress, insecurity, and fear is what it is, you open yourself to a different range of responses, not negative or positive, just responses. Your prefrontal cortex will be activated.

Think about the peace you give yourself or deprive yourself of based on the responses and reactions you make to the world around you.

Are you being open to possibility or are you caught in the trap of constant judgment? Are you the Chinese farmer or the neighbor?

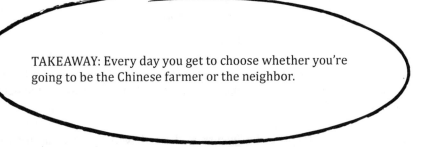

TAKEAWAY: Every day you get to choose whether you're going to be the Chinese farmer or the neighbor.

Lesson 26
E + R = O

*Between stimulus and response there is a space.
In that space is our power to choose our response.
In our response lies our growth and our freedom.*
∼ Viktor Frankl

*The great majority of emotional distress
we experience results from how we think about
ourselves and our circumstances, rather than the
circumstances themselves.*
∼ Thom Rutledge

Now let's take the ideas and lessons from the Chinese farmer and put them into a powerful, easy-to-remember tool that you can use to improve your emotional intelligence. First, we begin with these reminders:

- You choose what to believe.
- You choose what to pursue.
- You choose to say yes or no to people.
- You choose how to spend your time.
- You choose how to manage yourself.

Whether you realize it or not, you get to choose whether to respond or react to each and every event that happens. Events themselves are value neutral. They just "are."

The way you interpret the events will be driven by your assumptions, perceptions, fears, experiences, education, and so on. With a high degree of emotional intelligence, you will respond one way; with a low degree, you will react a different way.

I've been talking about events, responses, and outcomes a lot in this book. You may have realized that the key to most things in your life is in how you respond to events that happen around you.

It can all be summarized in this simple, powerful equation: E + R = O, where E is the Event that occurs, R is your Response to the Event, and O is the Outcome you're getting in your life. What Outcomes are you getting? Are you getting the Outcomes you want? Are you living the life you want?

If you want to change the Outcomes, you have to change your Responses.

While there may be several or numerous factors influencing your Outcomes, your Response to the Event may be the only thing in your control, the only thing you can change. You can't change the Event after it happens. You can't change other people.

But you can change the way you look at the Event and you can change your Response to people and things around you.

Improving your emotional intelligence helps expand the set of Responses you have in your toolkit and helps you get better Outcomes.

In the quote at the beginning of this lesson, Viktor Frankl essentially is saying you should draw out the length of your Response to Events.

When you draw out your Response time, you can formulate a more thoughtful Response rather than reacting instantaneously. You can reduce the impact of the amygdala and give yourself a chance to activate the prefrontal cortex.

When you know who you are and what you want, you can make better Responses and improve your Outcomes.

When you improve your Responses and your Outcomes, you improve your emotional intelligence and you change your life.

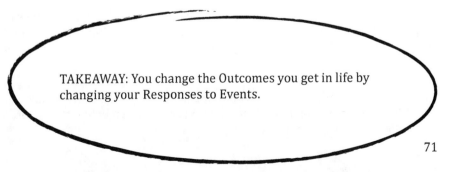

TAKEAWAY: You change the Outcomes you get in life by changing your Responses to Events.

Lesson 27
Triggers and Hot Buttons

> *Those who make conversations impossible,*
> *make escalation inevitable.*
> ~ Stefan Molyneux

> *Triggers are like little psychic explosions that*
> *crash through avoidance and bring the dissociated,*
> *avoided trauma suddenly, unexpectedly,*
> *back into consciousness.*
> ~ Carolyn Spring

One of the biggest issues to address when it comes to emotional intelligence are your triggers and hot buttons and those of other people.

When your triggers get activated and hot buttons get pushed, it's easy to lose control. They are typically related to things that happened in the past, their origins having little to do with the situation at hand.

The powerful equation discussed in the last lesson, $E + R = O$, is extremely useful in finding the best way to regulate your reactions. In order to use the equation to its greatest effect, you need to be clear about your triggers and hot buttons and those of other people.

One way to identify them easily is to increase your awareness when you say things like: "It makes me angry when…," "I feel offended when…," "I don't like it when people..," "If only people would…," "I get irritated when I come into work and…," and other such phrases.

When you use these phrases, stop and think about why the trigger happened. What is the feeling or emotion behind it? When did you feel like this before? What does the pattern look like?

In her book, *Getting to E.Q. Librium,* Yvette Bethel presents great questions for you to ponder about yourself, your reactions, and the underlying triggers and hot buttons. Here are some of those questions:

"Think about the times when people reacted extremely negatively or positively toward you and you were not sure why they reacted that way. What did you do to contribute to the reaction?

What are some of the things your coworkers say to you or about you in jest? They may lack the courage to have a direct conversation with you so they hide behind friendly banter.

Reflect on how you react when you are criticized. Do you listen, do you try to explain or defend your position?

Think about how you react to bad news. Do you become emotional? Do you prefer to avoid responding? Do you respond appropriately? How do you think you are being perceived in this state?

When you are in a heightened state of emotion/stress, you are sometimes only aware of your emotions, not the effect you are having on others. Take time to consider the impact you have on others while in this state.

We are sometimes unaware of the non-verbal cues we receive because we are so absorbed in our own situations. Pay attention to your coworkers' body language to determine whether they are reacting negatively to you.

If you trust a coworker, ask for feedback related to your strengths and your weaknesses. Who should you approach and how should you approach him or her?"

So, do you know what your triggers and buttons are? How about other people's? What reactions do you give when someone hits your triggers?

How do you handle your triggers and hot buttons? Well or not so good? Do your reactions add fuel to the fire? Do you lash out in a defensive way?

TAKEAWAY: Ponder where your triggers come from and reflect on the reactions you give when people activate them.

Lesson 28
Pulling the Right Lever

> *If the decision-making process is flawed and dysfunctional, decisions will go awry.*
> ~ Carly Fiorina

> *You can't make decisions based on fear and the possibility of what might happen.*
> ~ Michelle Obama

You can think of the Responses you give to Events around you as pulling levers. That is, when an Event happens, you will first decide if a lever needs to be pulled — if you must Respond — or no lever needs to be pulled. Many Events that happen simply don't require a Response: don't pull any lever.

If you decide that you must pull a lever — that you must Respond — the key question is what lever will you pull at what time and in what way in order to get the Outcome you want?

So often, you're faced with a relatively small issue, but you're triggered, in amygdala hijack, and you've gone beyond the point of self-control, so you opt to pull a big lever as your Response.

Other times, you're afraid of the possible Outcome, such as being embarrassed or making a mistake, so you pull a smaller lever than the situation calls for.

When you regularly pull disproportionate levers — whether too small or too big — you're probably having an emotional reaction that is packed with hurt, pain, and fears from the past that have been left unresolved. The lever you pull — the decision you make, the action you take — may not have anything at all to do with the situation at hand.

For example, one day, my wife ran out the door to work and within three minutes she was back. She explained how she had caught the front bumper of the car on a huge boulder as she was backing out of her parking space in our apartment complex. She ripped the bumper right off!

Instantly, in my mind I started reaching for the largest lever I could muster. I could feel my programming from the past start to boil. The fight-flight mode of my Sicilian volcano father was activated inside me. I had learned to look at life from a perspective of lack, that there's never enough, never enough money, never enough security. And this car situation triggered all of that.

What was rising inside of me was reflex, things I learned growing up; the lever I was reaching for wasn't based on any of the four pillars of emotional intelligence. Things were about to get emotionally violent.

My body tightened and a change had come over my face. Up to that moment, I had never yelled at my wife, but she could see what was coming.

She calmly said, "Whatever you're about to do, forget it. No one could possibly feel worse about this situation than I do. Besides, it's over. No amount of screaming is going to undo it."

Thankfully, I wasn't yet in amygdala hijack; she helped me instantly activate my prefrontal cortex and cool down the volcano.

After I dealt with the car issue, I reflected on the work I needed to do on my emotional intelligence. Why was I about to pull the biggest lever I could find?

Did I want to hurt my wife? Of course not. Did I want her to be mad at me for screaming at her? Of course not. Would screaming have helped to solve the problem? Of course not. Would screaming at her have been in alignment with my personal answers to the questions Who am I? What do I want? How am I going to get it? Of course not.

I had to understand that the lever I was looking to pull had nothing to do with my wife and everything to do with unresolved issues from the past.

TAKEAWAY: Pull the right lever in the right way at the right time to get the Outcomes you want.

Lesson 29
The Invisible Spectrum

*To be addicted to control is to be
endlessly out of control.*
> ~ Thom Rutledge

*On our own, our tendency to yield to
short-term temptations, and even to addictions,
may be too strong for our rational,
long-term planning.*
> ~ Peter Singer

Another way you can regulate your Responses to Events is to think in terms of what I call the invisible spectrum.

At every decision point in your life, an invisible spectrum appears over your head. One end of the spectrum is called "extreme positive"; the other end is "extreme negative."

You have the option to choose a spot on that spectrum as your Response; it can be at either of the extremes or anywhere in between. The most important question here is: Are your Responses giving you the Outcomes you really want in life?

Many times our low emotional intelligence, our fear, our need to protect ourselves, our narrative from the past drives the Responses we make.

Once, at a conference I was hosting, a participant stood up in front of the audience of 150 women and complained about something I had mismanaged in the conference.

Years later, when I was delivering a program on EI, I told the participants the story about the conference and asked for an example of what I could have said to the woman. One person said, "You could have said, 'Sit your ass down!'" Of course the participants laughed. And, yes, I could have said that.

What would I have gained? For a few seconds I might have felt good about putting that woman "in her place." After that, it would have been all downhill. At least some, if not many, in the audience would have been upset. Someone likely would have called my boss. I would have paid for that remark for days and possibly weeks or months afterwards. More importantly, had I given a reaction like that, I know it would have been driven by low emotional intelligence and fear.

There was no negative fallout from that experience because I chose the extreme positive Response. "Thank you so much for your input. I appreciate that. I'll look into it immediately."

Later, when I saw the woman in the hallway during a break, the same opportunity arose: either negative or positive Response. It was up to me and once again I chose positive.

We always have a choice. When someone starts yelling at you, you have a choice to make. Of course, it's not a pleasant experience, and you may choose to yell back. Your thinking might be something like, "That person made me so mad!" or "That person made me angry!"

As you consider your Response, you can ask yourself questions like, "Is that person's Response really about the issue or about his or her fear?" "Does the fact that this person has chosen to yell mean that I have to yell, too?"

The fact of the matter is no one forces you to argue. You choose. You choose to engage. You choose to raise your voice. You choose to believe everything is about you. You choose to believe that everything requires a Response. You choose to believe that people have so much power over you.

The right Response, for me, is the one that is not based in fear, and serves both me and the other person involved whenever possible.

> TAKEAWAY: Choose Responses that are aligned with your dreams, not your fears.

Lesson 30
Putting It All Together

*You don't have to attend every argument
you're invited to.*

~ Unknown

**If you care about what people think about you,
you will end up being their slave.
Reject and pull your own rope.**

~ Auliq Ice

The following vignette from the very informative book, *How to Talk So Teens Will Listen & Listen So Teens Will Talk*, by Adele Faber and Elaine Mazlish, is a great illustration of virtually all of the lessons to this point.

Here it is:

"I took my daughter shopping for jeans. Big mistake. Nothing she tried on was 'right.' It wasn't the right fit, or the right color, or the right designer label. Finally, she found a pair she liked — a low-cut, skin-tight number that she could barely zip up and that outlined every part of her bottom.

I didn't say a word. I just left her in the dressing room and went out to look for a larger size. When I came back, she was still admiring herself in the mirror. She took one look at the pants I held up for her and started yelling, 'I'm not trying those on! You want me to look like a nerd! Just because you're fat, you think everyone should wear big clothes. Well, I'm not gonna hide my body the way you do!'

I was so hurt, so angry, I came very close to calling her a little bitch. But I didn't. I said, 'I'll wait for you outside.' It was all I could manage.

She said, 'What about my jeans?'

I repeated, 'I'll wait for you outside,' and left her in the dressing room.

When she finally came out, the last thing I wanted to do was 'acknowledge her feelings,' but I did anyway. I said, 'I know you liked those jeans. And I know you're upset because I don't approve of them.' Then I let her know how I felt. 'When I'm spoken to that way, something in me shuts down. I don't feel like shopping anymore, or helping anymore, or even talking anymore.'

Neither one of us said anything on the whole ride home. But just before we got to the house, she mumbled, 'Sorry.'

It wasn't much of an apology, but still, I was glad to hear it. I was also glad I hadn't said anything to her that I would've had to apologize for."

Mom handled that difficult situation very well. It would have been easy to react instead of Respond, especially given the high degree of disrespect the daughter was showing.

When mom felt her buttons being pushed and her triggers being activated, she pushed the pause button by physically removing herself from the situation. She successfully tamped down the amygdala and activated the prefrontal cortex.

Perhaps instinctively she even understood that her daughter was being ruled by her limbic system in that moment and that a reasonable, measured Response from her daughter was unlikely due to a prefrontal cortex that is not yet fully developed.

Whether she realized it or not, mom became the Chinese farmer, essentially saying to herself, 'It is what it is. Now, what good can we bring from it?' Then, she created space between the Event and her Response in a wonderful exhibit of E + R = O, and got an Outcome that was so much better than the alternative.

Mom displayed an amazing amount of emotional intelligence!

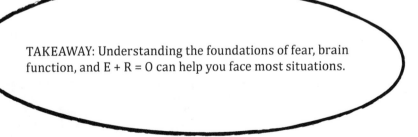

TAKEAWAY: Understanding the foundations of fear, brain function, and E + R = O can help you face most situations.

Part 5

Resilience and EI

Lesson 31
Resilience

*Man never made any material
as resilient as the human spirit.*

~ Bern William

*Resilient people immediately look at the problem
and say, "What's the solution to that?
What is this trying to teach me?"*

~ Jack Canfield

Why do some people make decisions out of fear and low EI while others make them out of intention and high EI? What's one major difference between those two approaches?

Resilience.

Resilience is the ability to bounce back in the face of hardship and adversity, and perform well on a consistent basis. Like a stress ball that returns to its original shape after being squeezed, the resilient recover more quickly when life's pressures mount.

People of high EI make good decisions and respond instead of react. When things go badly, they continue to make good decisions and continue to respond instead of react. In this way, they bounce back more easily than someone of low EI. Richard J. Davidson, Ph.D., the author of *The Emotional Life of Your Brain*, offers a great definition of resilience that lines up perfectly with earlier sections of this book: "By damping down the amygdala, the prefrontal cortex is able to quiet signals associated with negative emotions, enabling the brain to plan and act effectively without being distracted by negative emotion."

Ten psychological and social factors have been identified as making a person more resilient:

1. Facing fear
2. Having a moral compass
3. Drawing on faith
4. Using social support
5. Having good role models
6. Being physically fit
7. Making sure your brain is challenged
8. Having cognitive and emotional flexibility
9. Having meaning, purpose, and growth in life
10. Being optimistic

High emotional intelligence and the practice of being resilient help to reduce stress. There are four basic strategies for cultivating resilience in the face of daily stressors:

1. **Change your stressors.** Once you've experienced a stressor, it can't be reversed or prevented, but you can make adjustments so that future events don't cause stress. Identify the source of stress and then change your responses when it appears again.

2. **Remove yourself from your stressors.** After facing a difficult situation, you can take a few minutes for yourself to help release some pressure.

3. **Change your thinking.** This is the most powerful tool you have for increasing resilience. How you feel is a result of what you are thinking.

4. **Reduce the effects of stress.** Taking time for yourself, having fun, and balancing your work with a hefty dose of play are all great ways to reduce the effects of stress and increase resilience.

Each of these strategies helps you to improve your emotional intelligence, relax, decrease stress, and become more resilient.

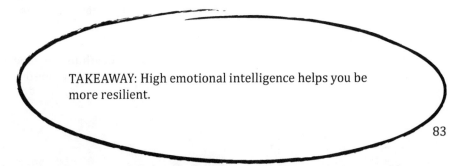

TAKEAWAY: High emotional intelligence helps you be more resilient.

Lesson 32
Resilience Inventory

> *Life doesn't get easier or more forgiving,*
> *we get stronger and more resilient.*
> ~ Steve Maraboli

> *The oak fought the wind and was broken,*
> *the willow bent when it must and survived.*
> ~ Robert Jordan

You may be wondering if you're fast or slow to recover from events that happen around you. In his book, *The Emotional Life of Your Brain*, Richard J. Davidson, Ph.D. presents a straightforward inventory that will help you understand yourself better when it comes to resilience.

"Answer each statement with True or False. If you're tempted to think long and hard about a question, or if you feel that there are too many nuances and exceptions, resist. The most accurate results come from making a snap judgment about whether a question is True or False about you.

1. If I have a minor disagreement with a close friend or spouse — closer to "No, it's your turn to do the dishes" than "You cheated on me?!" — it typically leaves me out of sorts for hours or longer.

2. If another driver uses the shoulder to zoom up to the front of a long line of traffic waiting to merge, I am likely to shake it off easily rather than fume about it for a long time.

3. When I have experienced profound grief, such as the death of someone close to me, it has interfered with my ability to function for many months.

4. If I make a mistake at work and get reprimanded for it, I can shrug it off and take it as a learning experience.

5. If I try a new restaurant and find that the food is awful and the service snooty, it ruins my whole evening.

6. If I'm stuck in traffic because of an accident up ahead, when I pass the bottleneck I typically floor it to vent my frustration but still seethe inside.

7. If my home water heater breaks, it doesn't affect my mood very much since I know I can just call a plumber and get it fixed.

8. If I meet a wonderful man/woman and ask if he/she would like to get together again, being told no typically puts me in a bad mood for hours or even days.

9. If I am being considered for an important professional award or promotion and it goes to someone I consider less qualified, I can usually move on quickly.

10. At a party, if I'm having a conversation with an interesting stranger and get completely tongue-tied when he/she asks me about myself, I tend to replay the conversation — this time including what I *should* have said — for hours or even days afterward.

Give yourself 1 point for each True answer to questions 1, 3, 5, 6, 8, 10; give yourself 0 points for each False answer.

Give yourself 1 point for each False answer to questions 2, 4, 7, and 9; score 0 points for each True answer.

Anything above 7 suggests you are Slow to Recover. If you scored below 3, you are Fast to Recover and thus quite resilient."

> TAKEAWAY: Finding out where you stand is a great first step to improving your resilience.

Lesson 33
Choose the Story of Your Life Wisely

Everyone is necessarily the hero of his own life story.
~ John Barth

Believe in yourself. Have faith in your abilities. Without a humble but reasonable confidence in your abilities, you cannot be successful or happy.
~ Norman Vincent Peale

Your ability to be resilient and have high EI is closely tied to what you think is true about yourself.

What is the story you choose to tell yourself about your life?

Is it one of hardship and struggle or one of accomplishment and joy? Do you tell yourself a story of self-pity and victimhood, making it more difficult to be resilient?

Do you like where you are or are you waiting for some future date to be happy?

For years, the story I told myself about my life was one of hardship and struggle. My parents didn't give me enough attention growing up. Nothing I did was ever good enough.

I was always in a hurry to get somewhere else, because, whatever was happening, *now* was no fun. And so I would rush around, tense and anxious, honking at anyone who got in my way (literally and figuratively).

This way of approaching the world — through my story of constant struggle, self-pity, and victimhood — caused regular disappointment. Nothing ever measured up to the way I thought things should look. Remember the gap between expectations and reality?

Disappointment, time urgency, procrastination, perfectionism, and guilt are some of the symptoms that arise from a story of negativity and self-doubt you tell yourself. Your EI is intimately connected to your story, and your story is intimately connected to your EI.

You live with your symptoms for so long that you overly identify with them, often believing that you are your symptoms, that you are your story.

You pride yourself on your perfectionism, not seeing how it erodes your happiness and increases the pressure you put on yourself and the world around you. You feel false satisfaction as you vent your anger and hostility, hoping to control the uncontrollable.

"I'm just an angry person," you declare. Or, "My perfectionism makes me better at my job," you think.

Instead of seeing things like chronic anger and perfectionism for what they really are — learned behaviors — you may identify with them too closely and take them on as unchangeable aspects of who you are.

But, you can unlearn some of your old habits, reframe your self-concept, and relax into a more desired behavior.

When I began slowing down, taking more time for myself, reflecting on my life, and realizing I had a choice about which story I could tell, beautiful things began to happen.

I saw that my life has been a series of amazing adventures aided by a cast of loving and supportive friends. I realized that my parents did the very best they could and I concluded that I had the best parents in the world. Everything from there on out is my responsibility.

TAKEAWAY: The way you tell your story matters and affects how you are now as you move into the future.

Lesson 34

Take Charge of Your Life

*If you change the way you look at things,
the things you look at change.*
~ Dr. Wayne Dyer

*Once you replace your negative thoughts with
positive ones, you'll start having positive results.*
~ Willie Nelson

As you realize by now, any and all personal change begins with a change in your beliefs and the way you think. This is worth repeating once more before you move forward because it's the core of everything you will encounter throughout the rest of the book.

Equally important to understand is that you can't change others; you can only influence them to make their own changes.

When you think about the things that aren't working out for you in your life, it's easy to start blaming others. "That supervisor's gunning for me!" you exclaim.

"They're always asking us to do more work! Don't they know how much work we're *already* doing?!" you gripe.

"These colleagues are trying my last nerve," you mutter, defeated.

The challenge with simply blaming others for your life is that there's nothing you can do about it except wait for them to change. "How long?" you ask. Who knows? That's not how personal change works.

It's your task to take 100% responsibility for the way *you* are thinking, feeling, and responding at any given moment. *You* have to take steps to change *your* outcomes instead of waiting for others.

Remember, E + R = O.

When I was younger, I did a pretty good job of blaming everyone and everything else for the bad outcomes I was getting in my life. I had terrible relationships. I was more than $200,000 in debt. I was overweight. I settled for "bare minimum" and "good enough."

Before anything external to me could change, I needed to shift my mindset, attitude, and outlook. I was so attached to my victimhood and my self-pity that I railed against everything.

Of course, I had become proficient at putting the best face on it so no one really knew what was going on inside of me. But, of course, I knew it...the same way you probably know that you're not getting the best outcomes for your own life and probably blaming it on everyone and everything other than you yourself.

One of the reasons I mention E + R = O so much is because it's powerful and effective. I used it to change my life. Just the same way you can use it to take charge of your life.

Whenever an Event would occur, I would immediately remind myself of the Outcomes that I want in my life. I reminded myself of the answers I gave to the three key questions: Who am I? What do I want? How am I going to get it?

I reminded myself so often that the Responses I gave became a habit, a positive knee-jerk response to the Events that happened around me. I remembered that other people had to take responsibility for their own thoughts and behaviors, not me. I remembered that not everything that happens requires a reaction from me. I remembered that I didn't need to feel guilty for other people's expectations or anxieties.

TAKEAWAY: When you take charge of your life, you unlock your personal power.

Lesson 35
Thinking in Advance

Worry is not preparation.
~ Cheri Huber

You can't solve a problem with the same mind that created it.
~ Albert Einstein

I often think about boot camps and training academies — the kinds of places where "thinking in advance" is taught.

Institutions like that are set up to provide as much training as possible so that when their personnel find themselves in difficult situations, they have a mindset and a guide for resolving them. Personnel are put through a wide variety of scenarios, and have the core principles of their organizations instilled in them.

It doesn't do anyone any good to start to learn how to solve a problem at the very moment it arises. Thinking in advance reduces uncertainty and fear so that you can keep your emotions in check when the situation turns tense or unpredictable.

Answering the questions Who am I? What do I want? and How am I going to get it? is part of thinking in advance. The more scenarios you imagine and decisions you make in advance, the easier it will be to face them when they arise, with focus on process and outcome rather than on fear.

Here's a simple example to illustrate this point:

Step 1: Acknowledge the context. You and your spouse grew up in households where there was a lot of yelling. Both of you know how it feels to live in an environment like that and don't want it.

You are both aware of the idea of Decide, Commit, Succeed.

Step 2: Decide. Both of you decide you don't want any yelling in your house. This is a great step, but it's not enough. There's no mechanism in place yet to strengthen your resolve.

Step 3: Commit. This is the important part. Commit to each other that there won't be yelling in the house *by not yelling*. Real commitment shows up in our actions.

You both commit by creating alternate Responses (E + R = O) to yelling. When the telltale signs of anger, stress, impatience, and frustration start to show themselves, you have already thought about your Response in advance.

Step 4: Succeed. When you choose an alternate Response in advance of the Event, it opens the possibility to create a totally different Outcome, a totally different environment.

When there is no yelling, there is more peace, which increases the possibility of dialogue.

When there's constructive dialogue and peaceful resolution of differences, there is less need to activate the intense fear that accompanies protecting our egos.

When there's less need to activate fear, your emotional intelligence improves.

When you actively use thinking in advance to its logical and fullest conclusion, something shifts. You realize there are alternatives. Relationships change. Fear changes. Your emotional intelligence changes. Life changes.

Thinking in advance can be used in virtually every aspect of your life, from what time you get up in the morning to the job you take to the life you lead.

But it's difficult to think in advance if you don't know what you want. (Who am I? What do I want? How am I going to get it?)

TAKEAWAY: Start thinking in advance about specific situations and the Responses you'll choose if the situation happens.

Lesson 36
Re-telling Your Story

This above all, to refuse to be a victim.
> ~ Margaret Atwood

To dare is to lose one's footing momentarily.
Not to dare, is to lose oneself.
> ~ Soren Kierkegaard

I've spent some time laying the foundation of emotional intelligence: the four pillars; ways to think about your past, present, and future; the three key questions to start answering in your life; and a powerful equation to help you change your Responses to get better Outcomes in life.

Now we have guidance that helps us jump off into the next stage: taking action.

People love stories. Just look at the success of Hollywood. A great story is built on well-developed characters, a gripping or poignant story we can relate to, and the profound transformation of the hero.

Well, guess what? You're a storyteller, too. You can choose to tell yourself and the world any story you want. What story have you been choosing to tell about yourself?

The story I chose to tell myself most often was one of anger, self-pity, and victimization, focusing on the things I didn't get in life. I wanted more attention and more affection and more togetherness delivered in a way that I wanted.

Naturally, I didn't know anything about mortgages, bills, or the stress of raising twelve children. As a child, I wasn't equipped to consider that my parents may have had their own desires, dreams, and goals that may have gone unfulfilled. I had little idea what they may have sacrificed for my sake.

Like most of us, I was interpreting what was happening around me at a time when I was not particularly good at interpreting such things. And I created the narrative of my life based on those interpretations. It was a narrative wrought with fear.

Over the years, I came to understand a couple of basic things:

First, everyone has their own narrative and own perspective on how life should be, and that's fine.

Second, we're all delicate and sensitive with our own needs and fears.

Third, I don't have to, and indeed can't, live by other people's interpretations of what my life should be.

Fourth, and the biggest realization of all: I'm the one who made up my original narrative and can change it anytime I want.

I reworked — and continue to rework — my narrative to focus on the positive messages of the past in order to re-create myself. I re-interpreted my childhood, my parents, and most everything else around me to put fear into perspective and improve my emotional intelligence.

I continue to face the brutal facts of my life and understand that I'm not perfect, can never be perfect, and will never be perfect.

I strive less often for the dramatic victory and the heroic acts that live at one extreme of my life. I try to stay out of negativity and pessimism, which are the other extreme of my life.

Now it's your turn. Put pen to paper and re-invent yourself. Rewrite the story of your life focusing on all of the positive things that have happened. Focus on your self-awareness, on facing the brutal facts, on owning what you have to own about your life, on forgiving others so you can free yourself.

TAKEAWAY: It's your story. Make it anything you want it to be.

Part 6

Improving Your EI

Lesson 37
EI and Stress

It's not stress that kills us, it is our reaction to it.
~ Hans Selye

*The greatest weapon against stress is
our ability to choose one thought over another.*
~ William James

As you can see, emotional intelligence is very closely connected to the amount of stress you experience in your life.

Think about Vinnie's temper, my behavior on the Chinese boat, the mom in the department store with her disrespectful daughter, and my argument with my sister about my laptop.

All of those events were born of stress, some kind of tension between the expectations we had in our minds about how a situation should unfold and reality as it actually occurred.

Fortunately, in the cases of the mom in the department store and me with my sister, the stress was transformed, put into perspective, managed, and dealt with in reasonable ways. Healthy approaches to those problems helped resolve them quickly.

In the cases of Vinnie with his temper and me on the Chinese boat, learning was a little more difficult.

Vinnie had been through tantrum after tantrum, essentially perpetuating a life filled with stress. He didn't know how to use emotional intelligence to transform his life. After the Chinese boat, I spent years in the same behavior pattern, stuck in low emotional intelligence.

You should be clear on this point: the stress created by the actual situation is not the problem. There will always be challenges and some degree of stress will accompany those challenges.

The real problem is prolonged stress due to low emotional intelligence, not knowing how to get better outcomes in your life.

That constant stress — exacerbated by poor diet, caffeine, sugar, bad sleep habits, humorlessness, and lack of exercise — fuels divorces, bankruptcies, heart attacks, and numerous other maladies and ailments.

When you don't know how to conduct your life using the pillars of emotional intelligence, stress stays with you. Triggers and hot buttons continue to be activated. Poor decision making continues to plague you.

High emotional intelligence, in its essence, is a stress buster. It helps you turn on the relaxation response and turn off the stress response. If you think that you will simply ignore stress, it won't go away. You must actively turn it off. There are numerous ways to turn off the stress response. Some tools and techniques are given in the following lessons; others are discussed in more detail in *Being Resilient: 50 Lessons on Leaving Chronic Stress Behind*, by Adam Timm and Joe Serio, Ph.D.

So, these tools and techniques can be thought of as emotional intelligence resources and also as stress management resources.

One thing you will be surprised about: once you make a commitment to improve your emotional intelligence, it won't take very long to see real change.

You will make progress more quickly because you'll have more clarity about who you are, what you want, and how you're going to get it.

You will think in advance about how to handle certain situations and how to interact with certain people.

You will decide whom to invite into your life and whom not to spend time on.

TAKEAWAY: Stress and emotional intelligence are two sides of the same coin.

Lesson 38
Stay Out of Your Thinking Traps

The world we have created is a product of our thinking; it cannot be changed without changing our thinking.

~ Albert Einstein

Begin challenging your own assumptions. Your assumptions are your windows to the world. Scrub them off every once in a while, or the light won't come in.

~ Alan Alda

Creating some space around your unconscious, and usually reflexive, thought processes is a good way to increase self-awareness and improve your emotional intelligence.

Once you enter that world of your thought processes, you will probably find that you currently are in less control than you think. So many of your thoughts are just habitual. You've reached the point where you're on autopilot, making the same decisions over and over.

You may have irrational thinking patterns or have a tendency to think in self-defeating ways most of the time. Certain patterns of thinking are so entrenched that you don't even realize you have them.

Thankfully, the process of bringing your irrational thinking patterns to the surface is relatively painless. Once you realize you have them, it becomes easier to deal with them.

There are ten primary patterns of irrational thinking we fall into. Which one(s) do you see yourself in?

1. **Black and white thinking:** "I have to do things perfectly, because anything less is a failure."
2. **Disqualifying the positives:** "Life feels like one disappointment after another."
3. **Negative self-labeling:** "I feel like a failure. I'm flawed. If people knew the real me, they wouldn't like me."
4. **Catastrophizing:** "If something is going to happen, it'll probably be the worst case scenario."
5. **Mind reading:** "I can tell people don't like me because of the way they behave."
6. **Should statements:** "I should've done better." "People should act differently."
7. **Excessive need for approval:** "I can only be happy if people like me. If someone is upset, it's probably my fault."
8. **Disqualifying the present:** "I'll relax later. First I have to rush to finish this."
9. **Dwelling on pain:** "If I dwell on why I'm unhappy and think about what went wrong, I'll figure things out and feel better."
10. **Pessimism:** "Life is a struggle." "The chips are stacked against me." "Those people have it better."

These thinking traps block the opportunity for improving your emotional intelligence. Negativity brings on more negative thoughts, and then you feel stuck.

Breaking out of the trap and into a space of possibility takes a bit of practice, and the next lesson offers a specific exercise for doing it.

TAKEAWAY: Identifying your habitual thinking helps to change your thoughts and decrease your stress.

Lesson 39
The Daily Thought Record

*Thoughts are shadows of our feelings —
always darker, emptier, simpler.*
～ Friedrich Nietzsche

*Such as are your habitual thoughts,
such also will be the character of your mind;
for the soul is dyed by the thoughts.*
～ Marcus Aurelius

When an Event happens in your life that causes an automatic cascade of negative thinking, which then causes a negative reaction, there's no space between the Event and the reaction. The Event and reaction happen virtually simultaneously, causing a negative Outcome.

Remember, E + R = O, and that between the Event and your healthy Response to the Event, you create space. With space, you have an opportunity to change your reaction to a Response.

When stressed or anxious, thoughts and feelings can swirl in your mind and seem overwhelming. Putting them down on paper helps you sort it all out and see things more clearly. The daily thought record takes about 15 minutes each day.

Daily Thought Record Exercise

1. Start by identifying a situation you wish you'd have handled better. Write the details of this situation down on a sheet of paper.

2. Looking at the situation, what thought first popped into your mind? This is probably an automatic thought you've had before. Check the list in the previous lesson for the irrational pattern behind the thought.

3. Now, see if you can source the negative belief. Did this thinking come from a particular situation or person? Is there a deep belief or fear driving your thinking? Write this down.

4. The next step is to challenge your thinking. Look for evidence both for and against the thought pattern. Be sure to see the whole picture. If your thinking trap is "disqualifying the positives," and feel like things never go your way, take a step back even further to identify a moment where things actually did go your way.

5. Consider the consequences. What are the short-term and long-term consequences if you continue to think negatively? Always thinking badly about yourself or your situation takes a gradual toll. What is the impact? Once you understand your negative thought pattern, you can shift into a healthier way of thinking.

6. What's an alternative way to think about this situation? Now, write down a positive belief and an affirmation that reflects these healthier thoughts.

7. What action can you take in the future to support your new thinking?

8. Now notice if you feel slightly better or optimistic. This step reaffirms that by changing your thinking you can change your mood.

Using this method as a daily practice for 30 days has been shown to make healthier thought patterns a more regular part of your day.

> TAKEAWAY: Changing your thoughts changes your mood, which improves your outlook and your emotional intelligence.

Lesson 40
Silence Your Inner Critic

Talk to yourself like you would to someone you love.
～ Brene Brown

Be careful how you are talking to yourself because you are listening.
～ Lisa M. Hayes

You feel the way you think. Don't think so? Have you ever gotten into a heated argument with someone and woken up the next morning with the exchange still lingering in your head? Like a dark cloud blocking out the sun, these thoughts can take you away from the brightness of the moment as you brood over what was said.

The best way to feel good, then, is to mind your thoughts.

A little self-criticism is a good thing. It can provide the motivation to improve some area of life, but excessive self-criticism can backfire. "I need to work out more" is much different than "I'm fat and ugly." When the criticism is particularly harsh, you get stuck. It's hard to see what actions to take when any action seems like it will only bring you more of the same.

What is the inner critic? It's that voice inside your head that wants you to be better, the part of you that is continually seeking to improve. Your inner critic started out with good intentions.

On another level, your inner critic can erode confidence, prevent you from doing the things you want to do, and help push you to burnout.

Other frequent negative thoughts offered by the inner critic include:

- "There's something wrong with you."
- "You're not good enough."
- "You're different from other people."
- "No one ever notices you."

How can you tell the difference between your inner critic and your true self? Notice how you feel when your inner critic kicks in. Do you feel a slight drop in energy or a tightness in your stomach or chest? It could mean that your inner critic is preventing you from seeing a better way of doing things.

Use this 4-step process to overcome your inner critic and start improving your EI:

Step 1: Identify what your inner critic is telling you. Acknowledge that this thought process is separate from your real point of view and that this thought loop is not a reflection of reality.

Step 2: To further differentiate yourself from the inner critic, write down these thoughts in the second person (as "you" statements). For example, a thought like "I can't get anything right. I'll never be successful," should be written as "You can't get anything right. You'll never be successful." Notice how hostile and untrue these "You" statements are.

Step 3: Respond to your inner critic by writing down a more realistic and compassionate viewpoint of yourself. "You always mess up," could be written as, "I may make mistakes, but I'm always improving." This isn't to build up your ego but to show yourself a kinder, more honest attitude.

Step 4: Don't act on the directives of your inner critic. Focus on who you are and what you aim to achieve. If your inner critic gets louder telling you to play small or not take chances, then play big and take chances.

As you get into the practice of refuting the untrue words of the inner critic and ignoring what this voice says, the voice gets smaller and smaller, affecting you less and less, paving the way to better emotional intelligence.

> TAKEAWAY: Put your inner critic in check for better emotional intelligence.

Lesson 41
What You Focus On Expands

*The worst times can be the best
if you think with positive energy.*
~ Domenico Dolce

*The people who live in a golden age usually
go around complaining how yellow everything looks.*
~ Randall Jarrell

Working while stuck in low emotional intelligence can leave a mark. When you're annoyed and frustrated, complaints come naturally. The talk around the water cooler begins to reflect this discontent as well. When you participate in the discussion, you get just as fired up as those involved, dragging yourself through someone else's mud. Misery loves company, doesn't it?

In these moments there is a great opportunity to choose. After all, if *you* don't protect your positivity, no one else will.

The field of positive psychology has shown a lot about what's possible when people orient their lives around positive things. Positive psychology is the scientific study of what makes life most worth living.

Instead of a focus on what's wrong, positive psychology teaches that what's good in life is not simply the absence of what's problematic. You can find things to be grateful for or happy about regardless of your life circumstances.

Studies in positive psychology have given new cause to believe in the power of positivity. A few of the findings:

- Happiness is a cause of good things in life. People who are satisfied with life eventually have even more reason to be satisfied, because happiness leads to desirable outcomes at school and work, fulfilling social relationships, and even good health and long life.

- Happiness, strength of character, and good social relationships are buffers against the damaging effects of disappointments and setbacks.

- Good days have common features: feeling autonomous, competent, and connected to others.

- The good life can be taught.

And more beautiful still is that joy and stress cannot coexist. When you're happy and joyful, the stress response turns off, decreasing the production of all those harmful stress hormones. Just smiling has been shown to speed the body's recovery after a stressful event. This gives even more power to having a good sense of humor!

So, positivity brings a focus to those things that make you happy. Happiness leads to good things, which lead to more good things, decreasing your stress levels. It's time to take your positive feelings more seriously!

Today, while you're at work, see how long you can maintain your happy-go-lucky attitude. If something gets you down, do something to pick yourself up. Take a short break away from your work and get outside. Skip down the sidewalk for a few steps — I bet you can't help but smile.

When you hit the break room and the topic of discussion is the same old depressing stuff, take your food somewhere else and listen to some good tunes instead. If you focus on the negative, the negative will expand into your life. If you focus on happy music or do a little happy dance, happiness will expand into your life. This will be a major contribution to improving your emotional intelligence and the outcomes you get in your life.

TAKEAWAY: What you focus on is what appears in your life.

Lesson 42
Laugh Whenever You Can

With the fearful strain that is on me night and day, if I did not laugh I should die.

~ Abraham Lincoln

And keep a sense of humor. It doesn't mean you have to tell jokes. If you can't think of anything else, when you're my age, take your clothes off and walk in front of a mirror. I guarantee you'll get a laugh.

~ Art Linkletter

By now, you see that stress and your emotional intelligence are intimately connected.

Keep in mind what I mentioned in the last lesson: Stress and joy cannot coexist.

When you're engaged in belly laughter, having a good time, the stress response is shut down. Because it reduces stress, laughter positively affects all aspects of being. Just smiling has been shown to lower stress levels.

Physiologically, laughter enhances your natural defenses against illness.

Mentally, it enhances problem-solving skills and offers new perspectives.

Emotionally, it elevates mood and counteracts depression symptoms.

Socially, laughter fosters better communication and improves cooperation and empathy between people.

Spiritually, it helps you build resilience to stress and teaches you to live in peace and be at peace with others.

Laughter helps defuse negative emotions that keep you locked down in low emotional intelligence. It's a release valve that calms tension, quiets the amygdala, and helps you to regain your composure so that you can make better decisions.

Laughter truly is the best medicine, as the old column in *Reader's Digest* always told us. The problem is, we don't laugh nearly enough. We're so serious! And if you've ever been the butt of a joke, the target of bullies, or on the receiving end of ill-willed sarcasm, you know that there's a difference between being laughed at and laughed with. So the type of humor counts, too.

How can you invite more positive humor into your life? Here are a few things that will help you bust a gut and reap the rewards of lightening up a bit.

- Love your smile, and love your laugh. Don't be afraid to show the world your smiling face and laugh out loud. I had one friend who would cover his mouth or keep his smile small because he didn't like his teeth. Another would hold back her laugh because she thought it sounded dorky.

- Seek out the funny. Spend time with funny people. Make it a daily task to laugh. YouTube, your pet, your funny friend, a comedy night — whatever! Pleasure-seeking is not a sometimes thing. Balance the seriousness of your work with the lightness of laughter.

- Play pretend. Do you remember building forts, going on expeditions in the back woods, or exploring with friends when you were a kid? Time disappeared, fun was the currency, and you had no choice but to be right where you were. Give yourself permission to play this week and tap into that childlike wonder again.

Laughter and good humor are infectious, just like negativity. Which would you like more of? Making it a point to counteract challenging moments in your day with a little levity is a practice that can change the overall tone of your entire day, week, or month.

TAKEAWAY: Laughter is a gateway to greater relaxation, better communication, and improved emotional intelligence.

Lesson 43
Move to Improve EI

*Those who think they have no time for exercise
will sooner or later have to find time for illness.*
> ~ Edward Stanley

*Physical fitness is not only one of the most important
keys to a healthy body, it is the basis of
dynamic and creative intellectual activity.*
> ~ John F. Kennedy

When our ancient ancestors roamed the plains searching for food, and they met a wolf or some other threat, physical activity was the natural response to this stress — fight, flight, or freeze, as I wrote about earlier.

Nowadays, when you have low emotional intelligence and get stressed easily, you most often continue to sit where you are — at your desk, in your car — raised blood pressure, stewing in the stress. There is no life-threatening event, but the stress hormones are activated nonetheless.

The body is designed to take action when stressed, and when you exercise, you receive the many benefits of this activity. Exercise is one of the simplest and most effective means of reducing your state of stress arousal and regaining balance in your body which can then help you re-activate your high emotional intelligence and not let the frustrations of life get to you.

It's not surprising that an unfit person might not handle emotions, stress, and decision making as well as someone who is fit and in good condition.

When confronted with stress, the body undergoes a number of changes. More oxygen is required, heart rate increases, muscles tense, blood pressure increases, and your ability to respond well suffers. Your emotional intelligence plummets.

Exercise improves and develops your capacity to handle stressful events. It increases production of endorphins, the body's feel-good drugs. It provides a safety valve for stress, helps shed unwanted pounds, and improves cardiovascular efficiency and metabolism. It also fights chronic fatigue and insomnia.

I know what you're thinking: *On top of everything else, now I have to turn into a fitness freak too?!*

No, you don't. So many people adopt an all-or-nothing mentality around exercise and fitness that prevents them from doing anything at all.

You don't have to start training for a marathon. You don't have to run. You don't have to compare yourself to others or to your old high-school self!

Research has shown that just 10 minutes of walking each day is enough to stimulate blood flow and allow you to begin enjoying all of the positive benefits of exercise that you've heard about. Commit to taking 10 minutes to walk each day for the next 2 weeks and see how you feel. You can always go back to the way things were.

With exercise you'll feel more relaxed, energized, and refreshed; you'll be better able to concentrate; and your sleep will improve. With all of those benefits, your emotional intelligence — your ability to understand your own emotions, those of others, and act accordingly — will be greatly enhanced.

With just a moderate amount of exercise, you can stave off the effects of stress and cure yourself of "sitting disease."

The American Cancer Society published a study in 2010 that followed over 123,000 people from 1993 to 2006. The study found that women who sat over six hours a day were 94% more likely to die younger than those who were physically active and sat less than three hours a day. Men who were inactive were 48% more likely to die younger.

TAKEAWAY: Get up and get active. You'll reduce stress and improve your emotional intelligence.

Lesson 44
Be a Sleeping Beauty

Without enough sleep,
we all become tall two-year-olds.

~ JoJo Jensen

To keep the body in good health is a duty...
otherwise we shall not be able to keep our mind
strong and clear.

~ Buddha

You may not think too readily about the connection between emotional intelligence and sleep. Just start to think about the relationships between fatigue and good decision making.

Sleep is one of the keys to having sufficient energy and discipline in getting what you want. You have to find what truly works in your life. My preference is to go to sleep early. On a perfect night, I'm headed to bed at 8:00 pm, read, watch TV, or talk with my wife. Asleep by 9:00 pm and up around 4:00 am.

I work on most of my writing projects before the rest of the world wakes up. The books add to my accomplishments as well as the bottom line of my company and hopefully are useful to readers.

When I talk about getting up at 4:00 am, my workshop audiences typically moan. And then I tell them about my wife. Jennifer hated to get up early. She was a champion sleeper on weekends, and had convinced herself she couldn't wake up early. Until she started writing a book.

She was so enthusiastic about the project that she looked forward to working on it.

On weekdays, Jenn would get up around 5:00 am and write for two hours before getting ready for work.

What did this do for her? It convinced her she could write a book. It increased her confidence. It changed her sleep pattern. It impacted her frustration level. It helped her say no to things she needed to say no to. It improved her emotional intelligence by shifting how she thought and felt about herself. It changed her self-awareness and her self-management.

Sleep may be a major issue in your life, influencing how you feel in the morning, your communication style, your ability to get to work on time, and your ability to make good decisions.

Yes, it is possible to wake up earlier. And if you think it's not, or you're convinced you can't, here are some ideas to try:

- Make small changes. Instead of convincing yourself you can't wake up an hour earlier each day, get up 15 minutes during the first week of your transition. Add more time in the second week.

- Go to sleep earlier. This one is easy to fudge and requires discipline. Set a specific time to be in bed. Turn off the television 30 minutes before your designated sleep time in order to start calming your mind.

- Break the snooze alarm habit. Put the alarm clock on the other side of the room, forcing yourself to get out of bed.

- Know what you will tackle first thing in the morning. Write your success list the night before. Choose your clothing the night before. Make your lunch the night before if you're taking it to work or school.

If waking up earlier doesn't work for you, then organize your life so that you go to bed later and wake up later. Either way, you need to think in advance about how you might create the optimal sleep time to support high emotional intelligence.

TAKEAWAY: Strategize about the best sleep time for you to effectively improve your emotional intelligence.

Lesson 45

Breathe

Nothing can bring you peace but yourself.
~ Ralph Waldo Emerson

There is more to life than increasing its speed.
~ Mahatma Gandhi

One of the most effective and potent steps you can take to keep your emotional intelligence high or to regain it quickly after a period of tension is to breathe deeply.

This may sound simplistic, but it works wonders. And not just because it feels good, but because it's based on the science of your body and mind.

In 1973, Dr. Herbert Benson, then Associate Professor of Medicine at Harvard Medical School, discovered that by using simple breathing techniques, one can elicit changes that decrease heart rate, lower metabolism, decrease breathing rate, enhance well-being, and bring the body into healthy balance.

Dr. Benson coined this body function the "relaxation response" — the converse of the stress response (fight, flight, freeze). There are four essential elements in turning on the relaxation response:

1. A quiet environment
2. An object of focus or attention
3. A passive attitude
4. A comfortable position

When used for 10-20 minutes once or twice daily, the relaxation response stops the body from producing stress hormones while calming rampant thoughts, ending fidgetiness and anxiety, and creating more space to breathe.

Let's be more explicit about what is actually happening inside your brain.

When you're calm, you have a functional IQ of about 100-120, and you'd be operating largely from your prefrontal cortex. Your cognitive state can be described as abstract or reflective.

When calm changes to alert, the primary area of the brain being engaged starts to shift from cortex to limbic. Your functional IQ moves into the 80-110 range and your cognitive state is now concrete or routine.

If your mental state moves from alert to alarm (stress!), your functional IQ continues to fall, hitting the 60-90 range. You're now fully in the limbic brain and becoming emotional and reactive.

Finally, with full-blown fear, you are now reactive and reflexive and have shifted solidly into your reptilian brain with a brutally low functional IQ of 50-70.

As you can see, the physical changes in your brain are real and impressive, and your ability to stay in the moment and make great decisions is plummeting.

When the mom in Lesson 30 walked away from her daughter in the department store, she waited in the car. She created space. She could then sit behind the wheel and breathe instead of focusing all of her emotion on how disrespectful her daughter was being.

That gave mom the chance to keep her functional IQ high, avoid amygdala hijack, and make good decisions. Ultimately, the relationship remained intact and the situation didn't devolve into a full-blown argument.

When you're mindful of your tension and can breathe deeply, you're ready to use your mind to release the tension you've been holding on to. Like setting down a bag of rocks you didn't know you were carrying, you can unravel the tension just by allowing for it.

TAKEAWAY: Relaxing the body relaxes the mind, instantly creating the opportunity for more space.

Lesson 46
Learn to Say No

If you don't value your time, neither will others.
~ Kim Garst

The number one reason people fail in life is because they listen to their friends, family, and neighbors.
~ Napoleon Hill

When I was getting my Ph.D., I knew a professor who said no to a lot of things. It was a bit awkward to be on the receiving end of his no, but that wasn't his concern.

I soon realized it was no coincidence that he produced countless articles, received numerous grants, and won every major award in his field. He knew that saying yes to the wrong things would take him away from his goals.

In this case, he was exhibiting high emotional intelligence. He had identified what he wanted and how he was going to get it. Knowing this, he could easily say no to people and projects that were not part of his plan. He was self-aware, had good self-management, was clear in his expression with people and so had good relationship management.

Do you have a hard time saying no to people? Saying yes to the wrong things comes from a variety of places:

- You say yes to the wrong things in order to avoid something you're afraid of or don't want to face, like a difficult project or unpleasant task. You later use this distraction as an excuse for not facing your task head on.

- You grew up in a family, school, community, or church that valued saying yes to anyone who needed your help. To say no, then, might mean you're not honoring the values instilled in you growing up and can often result in feelings of guilt.

- You want to be liked, accepted, and part of the tribe. You don't want to come across as less than friendly. If you say no, you may be ostracized or exiled. You may be rejected and left alone.

- You don't have clear priorities and goals or a plan to reach them. When you don't have a plan to get to a desired goal or outcome, it's much easier to say yes to anything that comes along.

How does it feel at the end of the day to have given your time and energy away to other people and you have done nothing for yourself? You may begin to resent it, which then may affect so many other things in your life, including your emotional intelligence.

1. Understand the Nature of the Beast

Do you know who you can say no to and who's a priority? If you say yes to everyone, then no one's a priority and you'll allow anyone and everyone take your time. Are you saying yes to everyone because of guilt feelings, wanting to be a hero, trying to prove your own self-worth?

2. Think in Advance

Think in advance about the Outcomes you want to see occur. Think in advance what you would say and how you would say it if someone wants your time. If you aren't sure how to do it, consult with a friend or colleague who's good at it.

3. Know Where You're Going

People high in emotional intelligence who get what they want are usually very good about knowing where they're going. They set themselves up for success by understanding their goals, why they're going after those goals, and the road ahead. Knowing where you're going reduces the temptation of saying yes when you really need to say no.

TAKEAWAY: Be clear about where you're going and firm in your resolve to say no when you need to.

Lesson 47

Love the Plateau

*Patience and perseverance have a magical effect
before which difficulties
disappear and obstacles vanish.*

~ John Quincy Adams

*Never give up, for that is just the place and time that
the tide will turn.*

~ Harriet Beecher Stowe

When you try something new, your first steps are frequently filled with mixed emotions. You set out on a steep learning curve and seem to be absorbing so much very quickly. It's exciting and fun.

At the same time, you can feel anxious, uncertain, clumsy, and filled with trepidation. After all, learning something new can be scary. It'll force you to leave your comfort zone.

After a while, though, it will seem you're not making as much progress as you had been. The excitement and novelty of your new venture starts to wear off, and you become frustrated when you hit a plateau.

While it may feel like you have stalled, this is actually a natural occurrence. Most of the time, you won't remain on a steady, upward path; there will be ebbs and flows in your progress.

The plateau — especially the first one — is where you may give in to your frustration and simply quit. This is what people with low emotional intelligence do.

With your mindset of frustration, impatience, and fear, healthy self-management can be a challenge. It can be difficult to realize that another leap of progress is waiting up ahead.

The trick is to understand that plateaus happen, and fairly often. You have to be prepared to silence the inner critic inside your head when it says, "See, I told you this was going to be impossible."

When successful people reach the plateau, they simply continue to work. They know that plateaus are an important part of the process of continuous learning.

Plateaus give your brain time to make sense of what you're working on, preparing you for the next leap of progress.

When I was first learning to play guitar, my fingers were clumsy and I couldn't make the chord changes very easily. I reminded myself to take my time, to expect obstacles, and to remember that if I do my best on a regular basis, I'd see a big jump in progress after some time on the plateau. That's exactly what happened.

In the past, I couldn't see this approach to things because my emotional intelligence was low. I would get frustrated easily and trigger the emotions from growing up: insecurity, incompetence, lack of confidence, lack of belief in myself.

I also realized that quitting on the plateau was about my fear. As soon as things got too difficult, I would begin to replay the old narrative in my mind about not being good enough, not being acceptable, and not being lovable.

Later, this translated into quitting relationships when they got difficult, running people off when I felt too vulnerable, letting my temper and defensiveness influence my decision making.

Knowing that plateaus are natural, necessary, and temporary will help you improve your emotional intelligence and continue on the path you set for yourself.

TAKEAWAY: Understand that staying on the plateau is an important part of improving your emotional intelligence.

Lesson 48

7 Steps to Emotional Intelligence

*Observe the space between your thoughts,
then observe the observer.*

~ Hamilton Boudreaux

*The real man smiles in trouble,
gathers strength from distress,
and grows brave by reflection.*

~ Thomas Paine

In her book, *The EQ Difference: A Powerful Plan for Putting Emotional Intelligence to Work*, Adele B. Lynn, provides a 7-step approach to improving emotional intelligence. I've listed it here with my own explanations.

Observe
- Observing yourself requires that you understand how you think, feel, and behave, and how you impact others. Observe yourself when you react to people and situations. Do you rush to judgment before you know all of the facts? Do you stereotype? Look honestly at how you think and interact with other people. Try to put yourself in their place and be more open and accepting of their perspectives and needs.

Interpret
- This helps you understand your common patterns when interacting with others. This is exactly what Vinnie had to understand in order to change his temper. Do you become upset every time there's a delay or something doesn't happen the way you want? Do you blame others or become angry at them, even when it's not their fault? The ability to stay calm and in control in difficult situations is highly valued — in the business world and outside it.

Pause
- As discussed earlier, the pause button is one of the most potent tools in your toolbox. It helps reduce the intensity of the amygdala, push nerve signals to the prefrontal cortex, and help you maintain a reasonably high functional IQ so you can Respond appropriately to Events that happen around you. The pause button creates the space in between the E and the R.

Direct
- When you're in the space created by the pause button, you get to choose how to direct your answer to the situation happening around you. Will you choose to react or will you choose to Respond? How you direct your answer will largely determine the Outcome you get. While it's tempting to blame everything and everyone for your life, you are 100% responsible for your life.

Reflect
- If you're like most people, you may be failing to reflect on situations after they happen. This is especially easy if you spent your energy reacting and activated your stress response instead of your relaxation response. Think about what went right and what you might need to do better next time. Reflect on whether you're really getting the things you want in life.

Celebrate
- Take time to celebrate your victories. It doesn't have to be loud and obnoxious. Just give yourself credit when you put into practice the techniques discussed throughout the book. Acknowledging that you did something well, especially if it's new or scary, is an important practice to get into. Don't discount your successes; celebrate them.

Repeat
- Once you have had victories improving your self-awareness, your self-management, your social awareness, and relationship management, you then have a sense of how to do it. Now, do it again. And again. And again. It won't be perfect, and you'll make mistakes. Learning anything worthwhile will take time, patience, and perseverance.

TAKEAWAY: A simple, structured approach to emotional intelligence will help you make rapid change.

Lesson 49
The 7 Habits of Highly Effective People

*The main thing is to keep
the main thing the main thing.*

~ Stephen Covey

*But until a person can say deeply and honestly,
'I am what I am today because of
the choices I made yesterday,' that person
cannot say, 'I choose otherwise.'*

~ Stephen Covey

In 1989, Stephen Covey published his personal growth classic, *The 7 Habits of Highly Effective People*. While it wasn't publicized as an emotional intelligence guide, it can help your EI dramatically if you integrate the habits into your life over time.

You would do well to read the book, memorize the habits, and start living them the best you can. When I started integrating the 7 habits into my life, everything changed.

Here's a preview:

Habit 1: Be Proactive

Take initiative in life by realizing your decisions are the primary determining factor for effectiveness in your life. Take responsibility for your choices and whatever victories or consequences that follow.

Habit 2: Begin with the End in Mind

Discover and clarify your character values and life goals. Envision the ideal characteristics for each of your various roles and relationships in life.

Habit 3: Put First Things First

Plan, prioritize, and execute your tasks based on importance rather than urgency. Evaluate whether your efforts exemplify your desired values, propel you toward goals, and enrich the roles and relationships you choose for yourself.

Habit 4: Think Win-Win

Genuinely strive for mutually beneficial solutions or agreements in your relationships. Value and respect people by understanding a "win" for all is ultimately a better long-term resolution than if only one person in the situation gets his way.

Habit 5: Seek First to Understand, Then to be Understood

Use empathetic listening to be genuinely influenced by a person, which compels them to reciprocate the listening and take an open mind to being influenced by you. This creates an atmosphere of caring, respect, and positive problem solving.

Habit 6: Synergize

Combine the strengths of people through positive teamwork, so as to achieve goals no one person could have done alone. Get the best performance out of a group of people through encouraging meaningful contribution, and modeling inspirational and supportive leadership.

Habit 7: Sharpen the Saw

Balance and renew your resources, energy, and health to create a sustainable, long-term, effective lifestyle.

TAKEAWAY: Use the 7 habits in conjunction with the suggestions in this book to change your life.

Lesson 50
Mindfulness

*In today's rush, we all think too much —
seek too much want too much —
and forget about the joy of just being.*

~ Eckhart Tolle

*The best way to capture moments is
to pay attention. This is how we cultivate
mindfulness. Mindfulness means being awake.
It means knowing what you are doing.*

~ Jon Kabat-Zinn

Mindfulness, simply put, is about slowing down and noticing.

When you don't slow down, it's exceedingly difficult to hear what your heart and mind are trying to tell you.

It's difficult to eat well, be healthy, exercise, laugh, and sleep enough.

It's very hard to look at yourself and improve your self-awareness if you don't try to reduce the noise of the world around you.

Mindfulness is being aware of what's happening in this present moment. Staying in the present moment helps reduce the urge to live in a past that is gone or a future that has not arrived.

Mindfulness is simply being aware of what is happening right now without wishing it were different.

Mindfulness is enjoying the pleasant without holding on when it changes.

Mindfulness is being with the unpleasant without fearing it will always be this way.

In *Three Steps to Mindfulness*, Kipp Hawley writes that mindfulness is "continuous, clear awareness of the present moment. Always returning, whether from an emotional outburst, an enjoyable fantasy, or a melancholy remembrance; always returning to this present moment."

The benefits of mindfulness in connection with EI are numerous and profound: recover quickly from stress; improve concentration, visualization, and meditation; increase your capacity to feel the emotional tone of a situation; suspend judgment and be slower to reaction or defensiveness; reassess and reinterpret knowledge, assumptions, and perceptions; access greater imagination and creativity, and much more.

One of the underlying themes in this and my other books is the realization and acceptance that everything is connected. The four pillars of EI form the foundation of and are intimately connected to your stress level, health, laughter, sleep, breathing, your fears, the way your brain operates, your resilience, the story you tell yourself about yourself, your time management, your finances, your relationships, and virtually everything else. These relationships are vast and symbiotic: they all affect each other.

Without mindfulness, it becomes more difficult to stay attuned to what's happening inside you and others.

It becomes more difficult to make good decisions.

It becomes more difficult to Respond to the world around you and get the kinds of Outcomes you really want.

It becomes more difficult to remember who you are, what you want, and how you're going to get it.

It becomes difficult to have high emotional intelligence.

TAKEAWAY: Mindfulness is the core to improving the four pillars of EI and changing your life.

The Road Ahead

*There is nothing either good or bad,
but thinking makes it so.*
~ William Shakespeare

We cannot tell what may happen to us in the strange medley of life. But we can decide what happens in us — how we can take it, what we do with it — and that is what really counts in the end.
~ Joseph Fort Newton

This may have been an emotional journey for you, and that's a good thing. Sometimes you need to detox from the unresolved emotions of the past that you didn't even realize have been driving your life until now.

But try not to get too overwhelmed by it all.

Don't think that you have to reinvent your life and do it in one day. Improving emotional intelligence is an ongoing, lifelong process. It's not just another task on your to-do list; it is a central part of your life. Take it one small step at a time.

What kind of life would you like to have?

What kinds of relationships are you looking for? What level of financial success would you like to have? What kind of physical shape would you like to be in?

All of this is driven by your emotional intelligence, by your self-awareness, your self-management, your social awareness, and your relationship management. It is driven by the three cornerstone questions: Who are you? What do you want? How are you going to get it?

The bottom line is right now you have a choice. You can put the book down and continue with your life, changing nothing. Or you can begin to improve your self-awareness and make better decisions about how your future will be.

Are you going to stay locked down in fear? Are you going to continue to blame everyone and everything around you for your Outcomes? Or are you going to Respond to the Events that happen around you to have more of the life you want?

Nothing in this book is rocket science. It's all very simple, but it's not easy. This journey requires that you look inside yourself and face the brutal facts about where you are in your life and how you ended up there.

If you blew past the exercises in this book, I challenge you to go back and do them. The more clarity you have around where you are now and where you're trying to go, the easier it will be to get there.

The journey very likely will be painful. There will be tears, regrets, self-blame, anger, frustration, and sadness. But there will also be joy, gratitude, and satisfaction.

I want to urge you to choose a new path forward, one in which you can have more peace, better relationships, better health, better outlook, and better results. You will be amazed by the journey!

Go for it! You'll be glad you did. I would love to hear your success stories. Please feel free to email me at joe@joeserio.com if you'd like to share your adventure.

The Takeaways

Lesson 1   Emotional intelligence drives the outcomes you get in life.

Lesson 2   Improving your self-awareness is the key first step in moving toward high emotional intelligence.

Lesson 3   Begin to answer the three cornerstone questions to improve your self-awareness.

Lesson 4   Low self-awareness greatly influences how you respond to events that happen around you.

Lesson 5   Use your awareness of yourself to improve your actions and get better results.

Lesson 6   You can change your self-management by hitting the pause button.

Lesson 7   Get outside yourself to better understand what drives other people.

Lesson 8   Effective social interaction requires being slower to judge yourself and others.

Lesson 9   Your ability to relate to and interact with other people is a source of your power and influence.

Lesson 10   Your ability to change from reacting to responding will improve your relationships.

Lesson 11   The three components are constantly interacting with each other, governed largely by your emotional intelligence.

Lesson 12   Do what people high in EI do in order to improve your own EI.

Lesson 13   Face the brutal facts about your emotional intelligence to improve your life.

Lesson 14   You get to choose every day who you are.

Lesson 15	Increasing your awareness of your fear will help improve your emotional intelligence.
Lesson 16	False fear may be keeping you from exploring the four pillars of emotional intelligence.
Lesson 17	The larger the gap between expectations and reality, the harder it is to maintain good emotional intelligence.
Lesson 18	It's time to change your perception of what you can handle.
Lesson 19	Managing your fear and moving forward is a key part of improving your emotional intelligence.
Lesson 20	Activities of the reptilian brain are fundamental to your survival.
Lesson 21	The amygdala plays a central role in triggering your emotional responses.
Lesson 22	The prefrontal cortex governs executive function and helps counteract the emotion of the limbic system and reptilian brain.
Lesson 23	Understanding and regulating the struggle between the prefrontal cortex and the amygdala is central to your emotional success.
Lesson 24	Emotional intelligence helps you regulate the extremes of fight, flight, or freeze so that you can make better responses.
Lesson 25	Every day you get to choose whether you're going to be the Chinese farmer or the neighbor.
Lesson 26	You change the Outcomes you get in life by changing your Responses to Events.
Lesson 27	Ponder where your triggers come from and reflect on the reactions you give when people activate them.
Lesson 28	Pull the right lever in the right way at the right time to get the Outcomes you want.
Lesson 29	Choose Responses that are aligned with your dreams, not your fears.

Lesson 30	Understanding the foundations of fear, brain function, and E + R = O can help you face most situations.
Lesson 31	High emotional intelligence helps you be more resilient.
Lesson 32	Finding out where you stand is a great first step to improving your resilience.
Lesson 33	The way you tell your story matters and affects how you are now as you move into the future.
Lesson 34	When you take charge of your life, you unlock your personal power.
Lesson 35	Start thinking in advance about specific situations and the Responses you'll choose if the situation happens.
Lesson 36	It's your story. Make it anything you want it to be.
Lesson 37	Stress and emotional intelligence are two sides of the same coin.
Lesson 38	Identifying your habitual thinking helps to change your thoughts and decrease your stress.
Lesson 39	Changing your thoughts changes your mood, which improves your outlook and your emotional intelligence.
Lesson 40	Put your inner critic in check for better emotional intelligence.
Lesson 41	What you focus on is what appears in your life.
Lesson 42	Laughter is a gateway to greater relaxation, better communication, and improved emotional intelligence.
Lesson 43	Get up and get active. You'll reduce stress and improve your emotional intelligence.
Lesson 44	Strategize about the best sleep time for you to effectively improve your emotional intelligence.
Lesson 45	Relaxing the body relaxes the mind, instantly creating the opportunity for more space.

Lesson 46	Be clear about where you're going and firm in your resolve to say no when you need to.
Lesson 47	Understand that staying on the plateau is an important part of improving your emotional intelligence.
Lesson 48	A simple, structured approach to emotional intelligence will help you make rapid change.
Lesson 49	Use the 7 habits in conjunction with the suggestions in this book to change your life.
Lesson 50	Mindfulness is the core to improving the four pillars of EI and changing your life.

Biography

Dr. Joe Serio is a popular and entertaining trainer and conference keynote speaker on leadership and change, time management and organizational skills, strategies for effective communication, and overcoming barriers to improved performance. He motivates and inspires his audiences while providing thought-provoking ideas.

Dr. Joe holds a Ph.D. in Criminal Justice with a specialization in Leadership and Organizational Behavior from Sam Houston State University (SHSU). As part of a unique internship program during graduate school at the University of Illinois at Chicago, Dr. Joe was the only American to work in the Organized Crime Control Department of the Soviet national police (MVD). During his stay in 1990-91, he conducted groundbreaking research on Soviet organized crime.

During this same period (1988-1993), Dr. Joe was the founding director of a summer study program at one of the five law schools in the People's Republic of China. The program included visits to Chinese prisons, neighborhood mediation committee meetings, courts, re-education through labor camps, and other criminal justice-related agencies.

In 1995-96, he worked as a Moscow-based consultant to the global corporate investigation and business intelligence firm, Kroll Associates. In 1997, he was named director of Kroll's Moscow office, where he managed a wide variety of investigations across the former Soviet Union and coordinated with Kroll offices around the world.

Dr. Joe is the author of the critically-acclaimed book, *Investigating the Russian Mafia*. He has delivered presentations to audiences in Russia, China, Canada, and the U.S. on Russian organized crime and security issues.

In the 1990s, he worked in Moscow as a media consultant to *The New York Times*, *The Washington Post*, CNN, BBC, and other media outlets. He helped produce three documentaries on Russian crime, including one inside Russian prisons, for the television program *Investigative Reports* on American cable channel A&E. He was also instrumental in producing the first-ever newspaper series on the Russian mafia. The eight-part series, "Glasnost Gangsters," appeared in the *Chicago Tribune* in 1991.

Dr. Joe also served for six years as Editor-in-Chief of the highly-regarded bi-monthly magazine, *Crime and Justice International*, which was produced at SHSU's Criminal Justice Center and distributed to more than 25 countries.

From 2013 to the present, Dr. Joe has been delivering conference keynote presentations to businesses, associations, and criminal justice agencies.

As a recorded musician, he occasionally brings music to his presentations, using harmonica and guitar to illustrate points pertaining to time management, organizational skills, and effective communication.

CPSIA information can be obtained
at www.ICGtesting.com
Printed in the USA
BVHW042349180219
540567BV00006B/17/P